CONVERSATIONS WITH
CLAUDE LÉVI-STRAUSS

CONVERSATIONS WITH
CLAUDE LÉVI-STRAUSS

Claude Lévi-Strauss

Didier Eribon

Translated by Paula Wissing

*

The University of Chicago Press

Chicago and London

Originally published as *De près et de loin,*
© Éditions Odile Jacob, 1988.

The University of Chicago Press, Chicago 60637
The University of Chicago Press, Ltd., London
© 1991 by The University of Chicago
All rights reserved. Published 1991
Printed in the United States of America
00 99 98 97 96 95 94 93 92 91   5 4 3 2 1

Library of Congress Cataloging-in-Publication Data

Lévi-Strauss, Claude.
     [De près et de loin. English]
     Conversations with Claude Lévi-Strauss / Claude Lévi-Strauss,
Didier Eribon : translated by Paula Wissing.
          p.   cm.
     Translation of: De près et de loin.
     Includes bibliographical references.
       ISBN 0-226-47475-5 (permanent paper)
       1. Lévi-Strauss, Claude—Interviews.   2. Anthropologist—France-
-Interviews.   3. Sociologists—France—Interviews.   4. Structural
anthropology.   5. Ethnology—Philosophy.   I. Eribon, Didier.
II. Title.
GN21.L4A513   1991   90-11052
301'.092 — dc20   CIP

∞ The paper used in this publication meets the mini-
mum requirements of the American National Standard
for Information Sciences—Permanence of Paper for
Printed Library Materials, ANSI Z39.48-1984.

Contents

Prologue

D.E. Did you always keep a journal or log like the one you quoted in *Tristes Tropiques*?[1]

C.L.-S. Of course, while I was in the field I used to take a lot of notes. Some passages in *Tristes Tropiques* are copied verbatim from them.

D.E. But you never kept a journal the way Malinowski did in his *Diary in the Strict Sense of the Term*?[2]

C.L.-S. My emotional states weren't that important to me!

D.E. I was asking you this because in *Tristes Tropiques* you maintain that you have a terrible memory . . .

C.L.-S. My memory is a self-destructive thief. It suppresses elements of my personal and professional life as I go, and later on I can't reconstruct the facts.

D.E. And to remedy that defect, if you indeed consider it one . . .

C.L.-S. . . . At any rate, it's extremely annoying.

D.E. . . . You were never tempted to keep a daily account of your actions and the events of your life?

C.L.-S. Never. Perhaps out of a kind of instinctive mistrust regarding what I do and who I am.

D.E. Mistrust?

C.L.-S. In *Tristes Tropiques* I said that I have a neolithic mind. I'm not the kind of person who can capitalize on or make what I've acquired bear fruit—instead I keep moving along an endlessly shifting

---

1. Claude Lévi-Strauss, *Tristes tropiques* (Paris: Plon, 1955); English edition, *Tristes Tropiques,* trans. John Weightman and Doreen Weightman (London: Jonathan Cape, 1973; New York: Atheneum, 1974).

2. Bronislaw Malinowski, *A Diary in the Strict Sense of the Term,* trans. Norbert Guterman (London: Routledge and Kegan Paul), 1967.

boundary. Only the work of the moment counts for me, and it is over very quickly. I don't have the inclination or the need to record my progress.

D.E. It is almost paradoxical to hear you say that only the moment and the event count for you.

C.L.-S. Subjectively speaking, that is what counts. But I get by when I work by accumulating notes—a bit about everything, ideas captured on the fly, summaries of what I have read, references, quotations. . . . And when I want to start a project, I pull a packet of notes out of their pigeonhole and deal them out like a deck of cards. This kind of operation, where chance plays a role, helps me revive my failing memory.[3]

3. We would like to thank Eva Kempinski, who, in addition to typing the manuscript, did so much to organize a transcription laden with additions, deletions, and corrections.

PART 1

WHEN DON QUIXOTE RETURNS

1

From Offenbach to Marx

D.E. You were born in Brussels in 1908.

C.L.-S. I was born there by chance. My father was a painter who specialized in portraits. Friends from his youth got him some business in Belgium, and he and his young wife moved to Brussels. I was born during that time. My parents returned to Paris when I was two months old.

D.E. They lived in Paris?

C.L.-S. My father was a Parisian. My mother, who was born in Verdun, grew up in Bayonne.

D.E. So you spent your childhood in Paris. In the sixteenth arrondissement, I believe?

C.L.-S. In a building that is still standing, 26 Rue Poussin, near the Porte d'Auteuil. When I go by, I see the balcony of the fifth-floor apartment where I spent the first twenty years of my life.

D.E. And today you live in the sixteenth as well. It must be a neighborhood you like.

C.L.-S. It's a part of the city I liked during my childhood because it was picturesque. I remember that you could still see a farm at the end of Rue Poussin, where it angles into Rue LaFontaine. Rue Raynouard was half countryside. At the same time there were artists' studios, small antique dealers. . . . Now the area bores me.

D.E. Your family had strong leanings toward the arts, didn't it?

C.L.-S. All the way back! My great-grandfather, my father's maternal grandfather, was named Isaac Strauss. He was born in Strasbourg in 1806 and came up to Paris, as they say, when he was quite young. He was a violinist and had started a small orchestra. He had a part in spreading the music of Beethoven, Mendelssohn, and a few others. In Paris he worked with Berlioz, who mentions him in his memoirs, and

also with Offenbach, for whom he wrote some of his famous qua-
drilles. In my family everyone knew Offenbach by heart. I heard his
music throughout my childhood.

Strauss became director of the court dance orchestra at the end of
the reign of Louis-Philippe. Then, under Napoleon III, in Vichy, he
organized the Casino orchestra, which he led for a long time. Then he
succeeded Musard as the head of the dance orchestra at the Paris Opera. At the same time he was a kind of Cousin Pons,[1] passionately
fond of antiques, which also were his business.

D.E. Has your family kept any of them?

C.L.-S. There was an important collection of Jewish antiques,
which today are in the Cluny Museum. Various objects that passed
through his hands were acquired by donors who gave them to the
Louvre. The remaining things were sold when he died or were distributed among his daughters. What was left was plundered by the
Germans during the Occupation. I have a few pieces: the bracelet Napoleon III gave to my great-grandmother as a token of thanks for her
hospitality at the Strauss villa in Vichy. The Strauss villa, where the
emperor stayed, is still standing. It became a bar or a restaurant, I'm
no longer sure which, but it has kept the name.

D.E. Was the memory of this past handed down in the family tradition?

C.L.-S. Of course, because it was a time of glory for the family—
they were close to the throne! My great-grandfather used to visit the
Princess Mathilde. My father's family lived with the memory of the
Second Empire, which was not so remote; as a child I even saw the
Empress Eugénie with my own eyes.

D.E. You told me your father was a painter.

C.L.-S. Yes, and two of my uncles as well. My paternal grandfather
started out prosperous but lost his fortune. As a result, when he died,
one of his sons—there were four boys and a girl—had to go to work
at a young age to help the family.

My father was sent to the Ecole des hautes études commerciales.
Once out of school, he began working at the Bourse in a lowly job.
He met Kahnweiler there, and they became friends. As soon as he

---

1. A character in the novel of Balzac by the same name.—Trans.

could, he turned to painting, which had been his passion since child-hood.

It also happens that my father and my mother were second cousins. In Bayonne, my mother's older sister married a painter who had his moment of fame, Henry Caro-Delvaille; another sister also married a painter, Gabriel Roby, who was Basque. Roby, who was of delicate health and died young, had an even more difficult life than my father.

Did my parents meet through family ties or artistic connections? I no longer remember. At any rate, before she married, my mother lived in Paris for a time with the Caro-Delvailles. She learned short-hand and typing to become a secretary.

D.E. Your father didn't make a lot of money as a painter.

C.L.-S. Less and less, as tastes changed.

D.E. So your childhood was not typical of the Parisian bourgeoi-sie?

C.L.-S. Culturally it was, living as we did in an artistic milieu. It was very rich intellectually. But there were struggles with material difficulties.

D.E. Do you have any definite memories of such periods?

C.L.-S. I remember the anxieties when there weren't any commis-sions. Then my father, who was a great improviser, would come up with all sorts of little projects. For a time the whole house became in-volved in printing fabrics. We carved linoleum blocks and smeared them with glue. We used to print designs on velvet on which we sprinkled metallic powders of various colors.

D.E. And you took part in these activities?

C.L.-S. I even created some of the designs! There was another time when my father made small Chinese-style tables of imitation lacquer. He also made lamps with cheap Japanese prints glued onto glass. Anything that would help pay the bills.

D.E. Have you kept any of his paintings?

C.L.-S. Not many. Because of all the pillaging, my parents didn't have a thing at the end of the war, not even a bed . . .

D.E. You mentioned the collection of Judaica assembled by your great-grandfather. Did your parents have any religious ties?

C.L.-S. My parents were complete unbelievers. But my mother, as a rabbi's daughter, had grown up in a different atmosphere.

D.E. Did you know your grandfather the rabbi?

C.L.-S. Very well. I lived at his home during the First World War. My mother and her sisters stayed with him with their children while their husbands were in the service.

D.E. Outside of that period when you lived with your grandfather, you were raised in a nonreligious atmosphere. . . . But was there perhaps a sense of Jewish tradition nonetheless?

C.L.-S. Not without its oddities. My paternal grandmother still practiced the faith. However, there was a touch of madness on that side of the family that would lie dormant only to appear in sometimes tragic, sometimes comic form. One of my father's brothers, who was obsessed with biblical exegesis and whose head was not set too firmly on his shoulders, committed suicide. I was three at the time. A long time before my birth, another one of my father's brothers was ordained as a priest to spite his parents after a disagreement. For a time the family counted among its members a Father Lévi. . . . I remember him later on—a minor functionary of the gas company, always quite dapper, with a blond up-turned moustache, smugly content with his person and station in life.

On my mother's side, my grandfather the rabbi was a holy man of a retiring disposition. The rites were scrupulously observed at his house. For three or four years in a row I was present for all the holy days. As for his wife, even their daughters doubted she was a believer. In Bayonne, she had put the girls in a school run by the nuns because it was the best in the area. The oldest daughter studied to enter the women's normal school at Sèvres, or even did enter—I no longer remember—at a time when the right-thinking citizens of Bayonne saw the women there as she-devils. The rabbi's wife had liberal ideas!

Although they were unbelievers, my parents were brought up with close ties to Jewish tradition. They did not keep the holy days, but they used to talk about them. At Versailles they gave me a bar mitzvah, obtaining my consent simply by saying I should not hurt my grandfather's feelings.

D.E. You were never troubled by religious feelings?

C.L.-S. If by religion you mean a relationship with a personal God, never.

D.E. Did this unbelief play a role in your intellectual development?

C.L.-S. I have no idea. As a teenager I was very intolerant on the subject. Today, after studying and teaching the history of religions—all kinds of religions—I am more respectful than I was at eighteen or twenty. And besides, even if I remain deaf to religious answers, I am more and more penetrated by the feeling that the cosmos, and man's place in the universe, surpasses and always will surpass our understanding. It happens that I get along better with believers than with out-and-out rationalists. At least the first have a sense of mystery—a mystery that the mind, it seems to me, is inherently incapable of solving. One has to be satisfied with the fact that scientific knowledge nibbles tirelessly away at its edges. But I know of nothing more stimulating or enriching than to try to follow this knowledge as a layman, being all the while aware that every advance raises new problems and that the task is unending.

D.E. Did you spend the entire period of the First World War with your grandfather in Versailles?

C.L.-S. From 1914 to 1918. That was when I started school, at the local elementary school; then I attended the Lycée Hoche. When we returned to Paris, I entered the Lycée Janson-de-Sailly in the sixth class.

D.E. Did you suffer a great deal because of the war?

C.L.-S. No. My father, who always was of delicate health, served in the auxiliary forces as an ambulance attendant at the military hospital in Versailles. One of my first cousins, who was much older than I and a brilliant student at the Ecole normale supérieure, was the only one close to me who was killed. Maurice Barrès cited and commented on his letters in *Les diverses familles spirituelles de la France*.

D.E. And so after the war you entered Janson-de-Sailly.

C.L.-S. I remained there until my examinations for the *baccalauréat*.

D.E. Did any of your professors there influence you?

C.L.-S. I don't think so. I found them more or less to my liking, but none of them took on the role of intellectual master.

D.E. So you made contact with Marx by another route?

C.L.-S. I mentioned my father's ties with a Belgian family. In fact, they were close friends; we spent all our vacations together. One summer they invited one of their friends, a militant young Belgian socialist who was already known in his country. I asked him about writers rarely mentioned in the curriculum at the lycée: Marx, Proud-hon. . . . He had me read them.

D.E. How old were you?

C.L.-S. Sixteen. And I was immediately fascinated by Marx.

D.E. Which of his works did you start with?

C.L.-S. I don't recall, but I began reading *Capital* soon after that.

D.E. You had no qualms about the difficulty.

C.L.-S. I didn't understand it all. In reality, what I discovered in Marx were other forms of thought also new to me: Kant, Hegel. . . .

D.E. Perhaps reading Marx steered you toward studying philo-sophy?

C.L.-S. I don't know. At any rate, I had a hard time at first in my phi-losophy class, and it was only during the year that I truly caught on.

D.E. What were your professor's philosophical preferences?

C.L.-S. He was a Bergsonian. A socialist and a Bergsonian.

D.E. Bergson never tempted you?

C.L.-S. No. I even felt hostility toward his philosophy, which seemed to give too much of a place to appearances, to immediate awareness. I understood more later one, and paid tribute to him in *Totemism.*[2]

D.E. You became a Marxist through this Belgian friend. But you also became a militant.

C.L.-S. He had converted me. Or was it a spontaneous inclination on my part? I can't say. But for a time he made me into a kind of ward of the Belgian worker's party. My first published work was printed by the press of the Belgian Worker's Party, L'Eglantine; it was a brochure on Gracchus Babeuf, the existence of which I would rather forget. And I became active within the French socialist party, which at the time was called the SFIO.

D.E. What were your family's political leanings?

C.L.-S. They were not politically active. On my mother's side, at the rabbi's house in Versailles, everyone was miles away from that sort of thing. On my father's side, they were a good bourgeois family that had seen better days, conservative in outlook. Except probably at the

---

2. Claude Lévi-Strauss, *Le Totémisme aujourd'hui* (Paris: Presses Universitaires de France, 1962); English edition, *Totemism,* trans. Rodney Needham (Boston: Beacon, 1963).

time of the Dreyfus affair. My father and his brother used to tell a story about going to a pro-Dreyfus demonstration where Jaurès was speaking. At the end they went up to thank him, and he said ambiguously: "I hope that you will remember this." Which meant, "You come over to our side but then immediately back off. " That was the exact truth.

D.E. You were extensively involved as a militant.

C.L.-S. I was the secretary of the socialist study group for the five Ecoles normales supérieures—though I attended none of them—and I was even general secretary of the federation of socialist students.

D.E. Do you still see any of the people you met at that time?

C.L.-S. Those I was closest to are all dead: Pierre Boivin, later on Georges Lefranc, with whom I had ceased to be in touch. I also knew Marcel Déat well.

D.E. Were you close to him?

C.L.-S. Not really. I knew him in the years before the *agrégation,* when to earn some money I was secretary for one of the socialist deputies, Georges Monnet. So I was often present at the Chambre des Députés when Marcel Déat was secretary of the socialist group.

D.E. What year was that?

C.L.-S. From 1928 to 1930. In the year of my *agrégation* I gave up the job because I didn't have the time.

D.E. Back to your studies. You left Janson after your philosophy course, and you began taking more philosophy courses.

C.L.-S. Because I didn't know what else to do.

D.E. The choice was purely negative?

C.L.-S. Yes. After Janson, I was at the Lycée Condorcet to take the preliminary course to prepare for admission to the Ecole normale supérieure. But I had no inclination for either Greek or mathematics, and I had to choose between them. So I began to study law.

D.E. Who was your philosophy professor at Condorcet for the preparatory course?

C.L.-S. André Cresson. When I decided to leave the course, he said to me, "Philosophy is not for you, but something close to it." And he suggested law. Indeed, it would be anthropology, but he had the right idea.

D.E. Where did you study law?

C.L.-S. At the Faculté de droit in Paris, which at the time was located on the Place du Panthéon and now has become part of the Sorbonne—Paris I, I believe.

D.E. How long were you there?

C.L.-S. Up to and through getting my degree. I earned a degree in philosophy at the same time.

D.E. Where?

C.L.-S. At the Sorbonne.

D.E. You did both at once?

C.L.-S. In those days law students often did not bother to take classes. You memorized the manuals. But law bored me to tears, and I fell back on philosophy. You see, these are still negative reasons.

D.E. And did any of the faculty there influence you?

C.L.-S. I am afraid to say no once more. It's not out of a spirit of criticism toward them but toward myself. I took Brunschvicg's courses but didn't understand a thing.

D.E. How long did you take them?

C.L.-S. For several years, until I took the *agrégation*.

D.E. Still without understanding anything?

C.L.-S. Still without feeling I truly understood! My professors included Albert Rivaud, Jean Laporte, Louis Bréhier, Léon Robin for Greek philosophy, Fauconnet and Bouglé for sociology, Abel Rey for history of science. . . . Basically, I went through it all rather like a zombie, with the feeling I was outside it all.

To show how little involved I felt: the very day the results of the *agrégation* were announced, I went into a bookstore to buy myself a book on astrology. Not that I believed in it, but as a kind of retaliation and to prove to myself that I hadn't lost my independence of mind.

D.E. You didn't take a great interest in your studies?

C.L.-S. Not at all. I had a passion for politics, for political thought. How did I pass the *agrégation?* It's a mystery. But I passed without any difficulty. I ranked third at my first attempt. It's a miracle for which I have two explanations. A very bright fellow student who was a devout Catholic had taken me under his wing—I believe he may have cherished some hope of my conversion. Greek was his strong point, and he had me prepare the texts. I don't know what became of him, but I owe him a lot. The second explanation is rather farcical. A doctor, a friend of the family, gave me a vial of some drug—morphine? cocaine?—which, he claimed, would give me a lift if I drank it before the lecture.[3] To prepare you for this supreme trial, they shut you up in the Sorbonne library for seven hours. I hastened to swallow the contents of the vial in a glass of water and became so sick that I had to spend the seven hours of preparation time stretched out on two chairs. Seven hours of seasickness! Further-more, the topic I had drawn from the lottery was the worst one could think of: "Is there such a thing as applied psychology?" Henri Wallon was a member of the jury, and such subjects were his specialty. I ap-peared before the jury looking like death, without having been able to prepare a thing, and improvised a lecture that was considered to be brilliant and in which I believe I spoke of nothing but Spinoza. After all, perhaps the drug had done its job.

D.E. Who else sat for the examination that year?

C.L.-S. Ferdinand Alquié, who ranked first. Also, among others, Simone Weil.

D.E. Did you know her well?

C.L.-S. That's putting it too strongly. We used to chat in the halls at the Sorbonne. The sharpness of her opinions baffled me. With her, it was always all or nothing.

I saw her later in the United States. She was there for awhile before she went to England, where she died. She called me and had me meet her at the entrance to a large building—the library at Columbia or the New York Public Library, I don't remember. We sat on the steps and talked. The women intellectuals of our generation were often ex-treme. I included her in that group. But Simone Weil followed this extremism until it destroyed her.

D.E. You went through your probation for the *agrégation* with Si-mone de Beauvoir and Maurice Merleau-Ponty.

C.L.-S. At the time, the probation preceded the examination. It was a pedagogical test lasting three weeks. By chance I ended up at Janson-de-Sailly with my former professor and Simone de Beauvoir and Maurice Merleau-Ponty. We took turns teaching the class.

D.E. Was that the first time you met them?

C.L.-S. Yes, and we immediately lost sight of one another for sev-eral years.

---

3. This is a one-hour lecture which the candidate must deliver in front of the jury.—C.L.-S.

D.E. Simone de Beauvoir evokes that episode in her memoirs. She writes about you, "[His] impassivity rather intimated me, but he used to turn it to good advantage. I thought it very funny when, in his detached voice, and with a deadpan expression on his face, he expounded to our audience the folly of the passions."[4]

C.L.-S. I have no recollection of it.

D.E. Did you get along well with her?

C.L.-S. I think so. I still have the memory of Simone de Beauvoir at that time: very young, with a fresh, bright complexion, like a little peasant girl. She had a crisp but sweet side to her, like a rosy apple.

D.E. And Merleau-Ponty?

C.L.-S. Since I knew him quite well later on, my earliest memories have been overshadowed.

D.E. In retrospect, this meeting for three weeks must seem very strange, almost premonitory?

C.L.-S. Above all it seems faraway, almost ghostlike.

D.E. You and Simone de Beauvoir never became friends?

C.L.-S. Never. But not because of any antagonism between us.

D.E. You never hit it off?

C.L.-S. That's not it, either. She and Sartre became famous so quickly; they held a much higher position than I in the intellectual world. They intimidated me and didn't need me. When Margaret Mead came to Paris—in 1949, I believe—I took the risk of introducing the First Lady of American intellectual life to the First Lady of French intellectual life. I gave a small reception in their honor. They didn't say a word to one another!

D.E. Because of the language barrier, perhaps?

C.L.-S. Perhaps. Each one remained in a corner of the room surrounded by her court.

D.E. You did your training for the *agrégation* together, but she passed in 1929, if I am to believe her memoirs, and you in 1931.

C.L.-S. The law degree took another year. And then I had additional work to help out with the family finances. Nonetheless, I passed before I turned twenty-three.

---

4. Simone de Beauvoir, *Mémoires d'une jeune fille rangée* (Paris: Gallimard, 1972); English edition, *Memoirs of a Dutiful Daughter,* trans. James Kirkup (New York: Harper and Row, 1958), p. 294.

When I learned the results, I rushed home in a taxi to give the good news to my parents, but an atmosphere of mourning pervaded the house. My father's last surviving brother was there. For a long time, a large sum of money that he had acquired through the stock market had enabled him to support his mother and to give my parents a hand in hard times. He was telling them that the slump had utterly ruined him financially. I found out almost simultaneously that I had a profession and that my parents' material needs would thereafter be a constant worry for me.

D.E. After the *agrégation,* you were appointed to teach in the lycée in Mont-de-Marsan.

C.L.-S. Not right away. First I did my military service. I was in Strasbourg for four months, and then, thanks to political connections, I was at the war ministry with a few other appointees, including Paul Gadenne.

D.E. Were you two friendly?

C.L.-S. No. He was a very courteous person but extremely reserved and unbending.

D.E. What did you do there?

C.L.-S. We were the press service for the minister. We read the papers and cut out what might interest him. The staff also entrusted us with any correspondence judged to be insignificant.

D.E. At that time you had given up all political activity?

C.L.-S. Of course. That would have been unacceptable. If you met General Weygand in a hallway without coming to attention, you were immediately stationed in a faraway garrison.

D.E. What images remain from this period of your life?

C.L.-S. Strasbourg left no unpleasant memories. I was a low-ranking soldier, but I met some amusing people there. And also, I found relatives there whom I hadn't known before. They stuffed my pockets with food. In Paris there was hardly any work; only one of us had to be on duty while the others went about their business.

D.E. And so after your military service you were appointed professor at the Mont-de-Marsan lycée?

C.L.-S. I had the choice between Aubusson and Mont-de-Marsan. I chose Mont-de-Marsan. It was both my first job and my honeymoon. I was married the day before I left.

D.E. And you moved there.

C.L.-S. I began my job October 1, 1932, and immediately became involved in local politics. I was a candidate in the cantonal elections. The whole business was cut short because I was in an automobile accident. I was driving without a license. My childhood friend and comrade from the socialist party, Pierre Dreyfus, who later became CEO of Renault and then minister of industry under François Mitterrand, bought me this used car, a small Citroën. He had driven the car up to Mont-de-Marsan, and we had gone off together to campaign. After an hour I landed the car in the ditch. It was the first day of the campaign and also the last.

D.E. How was this first year of teaching?

C.L.-S. Very good. It was my first year, and I enjoyed myself.

D.E. Did your political involvement affect the choice of subjects you taught?

C.L.-S. No, not at all! I was completely neutral in my teaching. For me, the two were completely separate. I didn't seek to convert my students. I was dealing with the curriculum and only the curriculum.

D.E. Do you have any memories of this stay in the Landes region?

C.L.-S. Memories of socialist circles more than of the lycée. Often political meetings were accompanied by parties with wonderful food. Those are the most exact memories. Others came back to me when I was elected to the Académie française. The little local paper looked up my former students and printed their recollections. Some of them wrote to me.

D.E. You were at Mont-de-Marsan for just a year?

C.L.-S. Then I was appointed to Laon. My wife, who had obtained her *agrégation,* was appointed to Amiens. We lived with my parents on Rue Poussin and tried to schedule our courses for the same days of the week.

D.E. And you began to find teaching less enjoyable?

C.L.-S. In fact, the second year I began to tire of it. And above all, I wanted to travel, to see the world.

D.E. And did you pursue your political activities in Laon?

C.L.-S. More in Paris than Laon, where I spent very little time. Even though the town, in its rough and austere way, was not without charm. The stocky, squat cathedral there is an arresting sight.

D.E. As in Mont-de-Marsan, you stayed only a year?

C.L.-S. A year and a few months. I left for Brazil in early 1935.

D.E. You told the story of your departure for Brazil in *Tristes Tropiques.*

C.L.-S. Yes. Célestin Bouglé had sent me to Georges Dumas, whom I already knew because I had taken courses of his at Sainte-Anne.[5] Dumas was putting the university mission together and agreed to include me.[6]

D.E. Your relationship with Bouglé had continued?

C.L.-S. He had directed the thesis I wrote for my degree.

D.E. What was the topic?

C.L.-S. It was called, I believe, "Les postulats philosophiques du matérialisme historique." It was about Marx, from a philosophical standpoint.

D.E. And you chose the subject yourself?

C.L.-S. Of course.

D.E. Was it usual at that time to study Marx?

C.L.-S. Rather unusual, but with Marx I had discovered a whole world, and I was under the spell of that revelation.

D.E. And you wanted to make him the focus of your study?

C.L.-S. I confess that at the time I saw myself becoming the philosopher of the socialist party.

D.E. When you think about it now, does the idea amuse you?

C.L.-S. No. I can't say that I feel any irony about it. The socialist party was a lively group where you could feel at ease. The idea of building a bridge between the great philosophical tradition—by that I mean Descartes, Leibniz, and Kant—and political thought as represented by Marx was very seductive. Even today I understand how I could have dreamed of it.

D.E. Bouglé accepted your subject without hesitation?

C.L.-S. Yes, but he balanced it with another. In addition to the thesis there was an oral examination on an assigned topic. Bouglé had chosen a question on Saint-Simonism; this was not too far from my own interests, but it required an orientation of them in a direction nearer to his own perspective.

D.E. Why did you choose Bouglé to direct your work?

5. A lunatic asylum. Georges Dumas was both a professor of psychology at the Sorbonne and a psychiatrist.—C.L.-S.

6. To teach in the university at São Paulo. See below, chap. 2.—TRANS.

C.L.-S. He was about the only one at the time who would accept such a topic. Indeed there was Fauconnet, but his work was evolving in a Durkheimian sense I found unappealing. Bouglé was the director of the Ecole normale at the time, and he looked down somewhat on those who weren't students there. Nevertheless, he accepted me. This explains why I let him know after the *agrégation* that I would like to go abroad.

D.E. Because he had official functions at the Quai d'Orsay?

C.L.-S. No, but in a way he was the protector of all the young sociologists.

D.E. And you wanted to be a sociologist?

C.L.-S. I wanted to be an anthropologist, and in those days the boundaries between sociology and anthropology had not been fixed.

D.E. Was it already typical for people who had passed the *agrégation* in philosophy to turn to other disciplines, to what today are called the human sciences, as would often be the case after the Second World War?

C.L.-S. It had begun to happen, although on a small scale.

D.E. Why had you decided to become an anthropologist?

C.L.-S. Let's say that it was a combination of circumstances. Since childhood I had a passion for exotic curios; my small savings all went to the secondhand shops.

In addition, toward 1930 it began to be known among the young philosophers that a discipline called anthropology existed and that it aspired to obtain official recognition. There was no chair in anthropology in the French universities, but the Institut d'Ethnologie had been founded, and the old Musée d'Ethnographie at Trocadéro was becoming the Musée de l'Homme. From that standpoint, things were moving. Jacques Soustelle was the first example of an *agrégé* in philosophy switching to anthropology.

Moreover, I read a couple of works by English and American anthropologists, particularly Robert Lowie's *Primitive Society,* that won me over because the theoretician and the fieldworker were combined. I was envisaging a way of reconciling my professional education with my taste for adventure. For as a child and adolescent how many expeditions had I launched in the French countryside and even in the Paris suburbs!

Finally, Paul Nizan, whom I had met two or three times at family gatherings (he had married one of my cousins), told me that he himself had been drawn to anthropology. That encouraged me.

D.E. What kind of a person was he?

C.L.-S. As far as I can remember, he was a bit cold and aloof in this bourgeois world that his marriage brought him into from time to time. Of course I had read *Aden-Arabie,* which I admired.

D.E. Did you read his other books?

C.L.-S. Yes, later on I read *Antoine Bloyé, Les Chiens de garde.*

D.E. A book like *Les Chiens de garde* must have made a strong impression on a young philosopher. Did it influence you?

C.L.-S. To the degree that it fit the framework of a Marxist critique of academic philosophy, yes. But I respected the masters he so vigorously attacked. For we had had the same teachers, a few years apart. I respected Brunschvicg, Laporte, Robin. . .

D.E. Why didn't you try to get to know Nizan better? It seems that you had a lot in common.

C.L.-S. He was older than I and never did anything to make himself more approachable. And then, with him as with others, I had the feeling of not being at his level. To give you an example: I would not have dared enter the Collège de France to take a class. In my eyes it was too prestigious, reserved for those more formidable than I.

2

Fieldwork

D.E. So in February 1935 you set sail from Marseilles, bound for São Paulo. It was Georges Dumas who enabled you to obtain a position in the university there. What were this great psychologist's connections with Brazil?

L.-S. There had been a strong French influence in Brazil since the late nineteenth century. French was a second language for educated Brazilians. George Dumas had gone there several times and had gotten to know the local aristocracy, especially in São Paulo. When the Brazilians wanted to establish a university in that city, naturally they turned to him to form a French teaching mission.

D.E. When was the university established?

C.L.-S. The year before I arrived. I was in the second batch of personnel.

D.E. In addition to the French, were there other foreign missions?

C.L.-S. There was an Italian mission, with, most notably, Ungaretti. I should say that there were large numbers of Italians in São Paulo. There were also some German professors, but they came on their own, for Hitler was already in power.

D.E. When you arrived, what was the atmosphere like at the university?

C.L.-S. The university had been founded by influential bourgeois at a time when tension between local power and the federal government still ran very high, to the point that it almost resulted in secession. The people of São Paulo saw themselves as the working arm of a nation slumbering in colonial torpor. These bourgeois aristocrats had decided to found a university to raise the local youth to the level of European culture.

But ironically, the students came from more modest backgrounds, for there was an enormous gap between the elite and the masses of society, who had remained in poverty and were provincial in their outlook. The students, often men and women already embarked on their professional lives, had little trust in the aristocrats who had founded the university. And we found ourselves caught between the two camps. While they considered us valuable, the students sometimes saw us as the servants of the ruling class.

D.E. Yet you weren't the "watch-dogs of the bourgeoisie"?

C.L.-S. No, but we had to be careful not to give that impression.

D.E. What were the courses like?

C.L.-S. The students had a colossal appetite for knowledge. Moreover, in a way they knew more than we did because, as they were self-taught, they had read everything, devoured everything, but in works presenting it second- or third-hand. Our task was not so much to teach them what they did not know as to give them an intellectual discipline.

D.E. Where was the university located?

C.L.-S. In the middle of town, in old buildings where you could breathe in the colonial atmosphere. Today the university, afflicted like so many others with a taste for the huge, is located in buildings of the style of the universities at Jussieu and Nanterre on a vast, rather stark campus.

D.E. How many students were there?

C.L.-S. A few dozen.

D.E. Which is a lot.

C.L.-S. Yes. It was the whole younger generation of São Paulo, or at least those who had any means at all. My colleagues who taught French literature had a much larger audience, for all of polite society came to hear them.

D.E. You were teaching sociology?

C.L.-S. That was the name of the chair.

D.E. But since sociology and anthropology weren't too clearly separated, you could teach anthropology?

C.L.-S. Don't forget that the Brazilian middle class had a long intellectual tradition dating back to Auguste Comte. His work had had an enormous influence on Brazil during the nineteenth century—the Brazilian flag even carries his phrase, *Ordem e progresso*.

D.E. Was this influence still felt?

C.L.-S. At the time there were still some very active positivist churches. But educated Brazilians had gone from Comte to Durkheim, who represented a modernized positivism for them. So they wanted sociology.

D.E. That must have been a bit difficult for you!

C.L.-S. I had gone to Brazil because I wanted to become an anthropologist. And I had been attracted by an anthropology very different from that of Durkheim, who was not a fieldworker, while I was learning about fieldwork through the English and the Americans. So I was in a false position. I had been brought in to keep alive the influence of France, on the one hand, and that of Comte and Durkheim, on the other. And here I was, at the time won over by anthropology of Anglo-American inspiration. This caused me serious problems.

D.E. Of what sort?

C.L.-S. The first year Georges Dumas had placed a young relative of his, who was a sociologist, at the university. When I arrived in turn as a new sociologist, the man attempted to put me in a subordinate position. This was not to my liking, and, as I resisted, he attempted to have me dismissed in the name of the Comtist tradition that he taught and that my courses betrayed. The ruling forces of the university, who were also those of the major newspaper, O Estado de São Paulo, lent him a sympathetic ear. If I remained in Brazil, it was thanks to the support of some colleagues who are no longer with us: Pierre Monbeig, as well as Fernand Braudel, who supported me with the authority he already carried. I recalled the fact in 1985 in the speech I gave when he received his sword after being elected to the Académie française. [1]

D.E. Although you remained in Brazil, you didn't leave right away to work among the Indians?

C.L.-S. At the end of the first academic year. Instead of returning to France, my wife and I went to the Mato Grosso among the Caduveo and Bororo tribes.[2] But I had already begun work on ethnographic projects with my students: on the city of São Paulo itself and on the

1. "Discours de Claude Lévi-Strauss," in Discours de réception de Fernand Braudel à l' Académie française et réponse de Maurice Druon (Paris: Arthaud, 1985), pp. 91–99.

2. The reader will find an account of his fieldwork among the Indians in Tristes Tropiques.

folklore of the surrounding areas, which particularly engaged my wife's attention.

D.E. Does anything remain of this work?

C.L.-S. Perhaps in the form of surveys that I assigned my students. A few days ago, I was somewhat surprised to see a bit of a documentary film we had shot at a rural festival. The Brazilians showed it at Beaubourg, with what survives of my documentary footage of the Caduveo and Bororo.

D.E. What were your impressions of your first experience in the field?

C.L.-S. I was in a state of intense intellectual excitement. I felt I was reliving the adventures of the first sixteenth-century explorers. I was discovering the New World for myself. Everything seemed mythical: the scenery, the plants, the animals. . . .

D.E. So you had a few months in the field and then a year of teaching. . .

C.L.-S. . . . and we went back to France for the next year's vacation. This was in 1936–37, during the Brazilian summer, which corresponds to our winter.

D.E. And it was at that time you organized your first exhibit. It was with the Musée de l'Homme?

C.L.-S. It wasn't quite the Musée de l'Homme, because they were rebuilding the old Trocadéro for the 1937 exposition, and everything was under construction. Georges-Henri Rivière, whom I met for the first time, persuaded the Wildenstein Gallery, at the corner of the Rue du Faubourg-Saint-Honoré and Rue La Boétie, to let the museum use their space.

D.E. What was in the collection you and your wife had brought back with you?

C.L.-S. It was a good ethnographic collection—I can say that, now that I have some basis for comparison. Among the Caduveo we had found decorated pottery and hides painted with motifs found nowhere else in America. The Bororo objects comprised mostly ornaments made of feathers and animal teeth and claws, for the Bororo richly ornament even their hunting weapons and their utensils. There were some spectacular pieces.

D.E. What kind of reception did you get?

C.L.-S. A polite appraisal. But I think it attracted notice, in any case.

D.E. And you became friends with Georges-Henri Rivière?

C.L.-S. Not at the time, for I went back to Brazil at the end of the vacation. When I returned to France for good, there was the mobilization, then war. . . . Then came my departure for the United States. I only became friendly with Rivière in 1949 or 1950.

D.E. When you went back to Brazil after the winter of 1936–37, you did not return to teaching.

C.L.-S. I had to establish myself as an anthropologist, for I had no formal training in the area. Thanks to the 1936 exhibit, I obtained assistance from the Musée de l'Homme and what was to become the Centre National de la Recherche Scientifique. That money made it possible for me to organize my expedition to the Nambikwara.

D.E. A trip that lasted more than a year.

C.L.-S. I didn't return to France until the beginning of 1939.

D.E. It requires a great deal of courage and physical stamina to carry out this sort of expedition. In *Tristes Tropiques* you write of riding over impossible terrain, crossing rivers, traveling by canoe. . . .

C.L.-S. When you're young, you have that kind of endurance.

D.E. When I read your books, I still had the impression that your endurance was of a special kind.

C.L.-S. I don't think so. But it's true that I never was sick. I was protected above all, as often has been the case throughout my life, by my lack of imagination.

D.E. An unawareness of the danger?

C.L.-S. Exactly.

D.E. Sometimes, however, you seemed to have been very frightened.

C.L.-S. I was frightened afterwards. At the time, I didn't realize it. In any case, we musn't exaggerate—I don't believe I actually risked my life very often.

*

D.E. As you said earlier, you met Fernand Braudel in Brazil.

C.L.-S. Yes, he arrived the year after I did.

D.E. Did you meet him as soon as he arrived?

C.L.-S. Of course. The French professors formed a small community.

D.E. How did the meeting go?

C.L.-S. Braudel was sure of himself, he was older, and had a higher place in the university hierarchy.

D.E. But he wasn't yet famous at the time?

C.L.-S. He was going to be famous. We knew that he was already headed for a successful career. He was an elder, more advanced in his career and in his thesis than we were. He hadn't written it yet, but he had the materials with him. Before he rented his house he had to have an extra hotel room for his papers!

D.E. Why did he go to Brazil?

C.L.-S. I think that for anyone interested in the Mediterrean and the Iberian peninsula, it would be important to know something of Latin America, as it was a former province.

D.E. You were not terribly close, it seems?

C.L.-S. He was a bit patronizing. Though when I had the problems I mentioned awhile ago, he did everything he could to help me.

D.E. Did the two of you ever talk about each other's work?

C.L.-S. I was telling you that as colleagues we formed a small group, but I should add that there was no cohesion. All of us thought our careers were riding on our success or failure in Brazil, so we all attempted to surround ourselves with an exclusive court, more important than our neighbor's. It was very French, very academic, but there in the tropics, it was a little ridiculous and not very healthy.

D.E. And did you know Ungaretti?

C.L.-S. Barely. What went on within the French community was magnified in the relations between the different missions. We felt we were competing and were careful about socializing.

D.E. You left Brazil in 1939.

C.L.-S. At the beginning of the year. I wanted to go back to France with my expedition materials, return to university life, write a thesis. . . .

D.E. And you never returned to Brazil after that.

C.L.-S. Never, until 1985.

D.E. When you went with François Mitterrand.

C.L.-S. Only for a few days.

D.E. Before you went back, didn't you feel any nostalgia for the country you had loved so much?

C.L.-S. Obviously. But I knew that everything there was changing so rapidly that if I went back I would only mourn my past. And that, moreover, is what happened when I saw Brazil again half a century later.

D.E. During your stay in Brazil, between 1935 and 1939, did you write any articles?

C.L.-S. A big article on the Bororo, which appeared in the *Journal de la Société des Américanistes*. And several minor pieces for various journals.

D.E. And you were never tempted to write a book based on your field experiences?

C.L.-S. At the time I felt incapable of writing a book.

D.E. Nonetheless, when you returned to France you already had several publications.

C.L.-S. Yes, but other than the article on the Bororo, there was not much. It was more journalism than anthropology.

D.E. Did these articles receive any attention?

C.L.-S. The article on the Bororo made it possible for me to go to the United States. It caught the attention of Alfred Métraux and Robert Lowie, who played a key role in my being able to go.

D.E. In fact, even your earliest work attracted some notice.

C.L.-S. Yes, but that is due less to my slim merit than to a combination of circumstances. American anthropologists were beginning to think that they had looked at all the Indians of North America and it was time to find something else. They looked south. My work came at the right time.

D.E. When you returned to France, didn't you have a place waiting for you at the university?

C.L.-S. I was still on leave. I requested a position for the following year.

D.E. You didn't think of taking a position immediately?

C.L.-S. I had to install my collections at the Musée de l'Homme and make out a card for each object, a long and arduous task.

D.E. What were these collections like?

C.L.-S. Abundant, but less spectacular than the first. The exhibit never took place. While I was classifying and analyzing the collection, the war broke out. This was also the time that my first wife, Dina, and I were separated.

3

Bohemian Life in New York

D.E. You were drafted.

C.L.-S. I had finished my military service in the Army Service Corps. So my first assignment was censoring telegrams for the postal ministry. I spent several months at that, but I was bored and requested to be trained as a liaison agent for the British expeditionary corps. First they sent me to school somewhere on the Somme, and then I took some tests. My English was rudimentary, but I passed all the same. They sent me to the Luxembourg border behind the Maginot Line, where the British soldiers hadn't yet arrived but were anticipated. I was there with three or four agents to meet them when they came. There was nothing to do. I used to take walks in the country to pass the time.

Finally, when the German offensive started, a Scots regiment arrived. But they brought their own liaison agents. Their orders came for the front, and they politely dismissed us—two sets of liaison agents would have slowed them down. It probably saved our lives, for the regiment was decimated a few days later.

Left to own devices, we set off looking for our corps. We found them at last in a village in the Sarthe. As the Germans were advancing, we were all put on a train headed for Bordeaux. The train zigzagged across France because of a disagreement I was to learn about only later. Apparently the chief officer wanted to follow orders and was ready to give his men up to the Germans, who were already in Bordeaux. His officers were against it, which made for the chaotic trip. Finally, the train stopped at Béziers.

D.E. So you never saw active combat?

C.L.-S. No. Except when strafing broke some tiles over my head, I was never exposed to the fighting.

D.E. And what did you do once you were in Béziers?

C.L.-S. We were quartered on the Larzac plateau. I was practically at home, since at the time my parents had owned a little house in the Cévennes for about twelve years. Then we ended up at Montpellier.

D.E. And what happened there?

C.L.-S. I took off from the barracks and went to the rector's office at the university to offer my services in case they needed an examiner in philosophy for the baccalaureat examinations that were about to begin. The timing was perfect, and I was demobilized a few days early.

D.E. And did you stay in Montpellier?

C.L.-S. No, I went to stay with my parents, who had fled to their house in the Cévennes. That was where the letters came from the United States inviting me to take advantage of a plan organized by the Rockefeller Foundation to save European intellectuals. Before that, in September 1940, utterly oblivious, I had gone to Vichy to ask to be reassigned to my job at the Lycée Henri IV, where I had been appointed. The ministry of public instruction was housed in a school. I was greeted by the director of secondary education in the classroom he used as an office. He told me that he would not send someone with my name to Paris.

D.E. Looking back on it, it seems incredible that you would have done that. Was the situation so unclear to the people who were living through it?

C.L.-S. As I told you, I never had any imagination. That helped me during my fieldwork — I was unaware of the danger. Well, this was the same. But the die was probably cast at that time.

D.E. So people were unaware of the gravity of the situation for the Jews?

C.L.-S. Perhaps some knew — at least the high official I saw did. I wanted to return to Paris simply to fulfill my professional obligations.

D.E. And what did the administrator who forbade you to go Paris advise you to do?

C.L.-S. He told me to go back to the Cévennes and I would receive another assignment. In fact, a few days later I was appointed professor at what was at the time the *collège* and is now the lycée in Perpignan.

D.E. Did you go?

C.L.-S. Of course. I was beginning to see that things were not going well because already there was talk about racial laws. The

attitude of my new colleagues was a sign. They avoided all conversations with me on the subject. Only the physical education teacher
was bent on showing me his sympathies—probably he was a future
member of the resistance.

After a couple of weeks I was given a new appointment in Montpellier. I taught a philosophy class and a preparatory class for the
Ecole polytechnique. The preparatory course was a lark, for the can-
didates for the Polytechnique couldn't have cared less about the two
hours of philosophy inflicted on them each week. They paid no attention to me. I played my part and taught my course in the midst of all
the uproar. . .

D.E. As if they weren't there?

C.L.-S. Just like that. This little game lasted only three weeks because I was hit with the racial laws and lost my job. So I went back to
the Cévennes.

D.E. How did they fire you?

C.L.-S. I got a letter. You had the right to your salary for a time
proportional to your years of service. After I went to the United
States, it kept my parents going.

So there I was in the Cévennes, where the correspondence with
the United States began.

D.E. Were you already in touch with American anthropologists?

C.L.-S. Yes, with Alfred Métraux, who was Swiss but living in the
United States, and with Robert Lowie, who was interested in my
work on the Bororo. Moreover, I had an aunt over there, Henry Caro-
Delvaille's widow. She went to a lot of trouble. Thanks to their con-
certed efforts, I received an invitation from the New School for Social
Research.

D.E. What kind of a place was it?

C.L.-S. Oriented to the left, the way the term was understood at
the time in the United States, and it had become a kind of university
for adults. The students came nights after work to complete their education. After the fascists took power in Italy, and then the Nazis in
Germany, the Rockefeller Foundation embarked on a plan to save
threatened intellectuals. Now they were extending it to France. The
New School served as a welcoming center and triage station, giving
the new arrivals time to find work at other institutions. Some of
them, moreover, preferred to stay there.

D.E. When the invitation came, did you immediately decide to leave?

C.L.-S. This was after I had failed in my attempt to return to Brazil. In *Tristes Tropiques* I told how the ambassador, who wanted to issue me a visa, was blocked by one of his advisors.

D.E. Why did you prefer Brazil?

C.L.-S. I had no preference. This happened before I was invited to the United States.

D.E. Was it easy for you to get your visa for the United States?

C.L.-S. Nothing is more complicated than being admitted as an immigrant into the United States. There were mountains of paperwork. You had to prove you had a job, an organization had to furnish proof that you were indeed going to be working there. You also had to find someone willing to pay a rather substantial fee on your behalf.

D.E. Who paid that sum for you?

C.L.-S. A rich American woman who happened to be a friend of my aunt.

D.E. And what needed to be done before the formalities in the United States?

C.L.-S. You had to have an exit visa, granted by the French authorities. No problems there—they were just as happy to be rid of people in sticky situations. Above all, you had to find a ship.

D.E. An on board this ship. . . .

C.L.-S. It was called the *Capitaine Paul-Lemerle*. On board were Anna Seghers, André Breton, Victor Serge. . . .

D.E. Did you get to know them during the crossing?

C.L.-S. As time went on. I was unaware André Breton was aboard. During a stop in Morocco, where only the French passengers were permitted to land, I was waiting in line to show my passport and heard him give his name, right in front of me.

D.E. In those days he was quite well known.

C.L.-S. Yes, so you can imagine how startled I was. I introduced myself and we hit it off.

D.E. Was he a friendly person?

C.L.-S. That's not the word. He was extremely courteous, of course, but there was always a certain regal aloofness about him.

D.E. Even there?

C.L.-S. Yes. He always had a very dignified demeanor.

D.E. And Victor Serge?

C.L.-S. We talked a bit about this and that, but I can't say we became friends. A few years ago when I was in Mexico I saw his son, who was on the ship as a child.

D.E. It was an impressive list of passengers.

C.L.-S. There were other people on board who later became famous. In *Tristes Tropiques* I talk about how the passengers were confined to the hold. Since I had patronized the same company when I went to Brazil, they did me the kindness of giving me a bed in one of the two cabins. Another bed was occupied by an odd character who said he was Tunisian. One day he showed me a Degas he was carrying in his suitcase. He enjoyed special privileges, and when we came to port he had no problem in going ashore. He came and went as he pleased. I knew his name: Smadja. He intrigued me. A long time afterward, when the founder of the newspaper *Combat* died and the papers printed his photo, I recognized it. It was he. He was probably on a more or less secret mission at the time, I have no idea for whom.

D.E. This was also when you met Soustelle.

C.L.-S. I had met him in 1936, when I brought my first collections back from Brazil. Now, after leaving Martinique, I was able to catch a Swedish banana boat to Puerto Rico, where the American authorities decreed that my papers weren't in order. They put me under surveillance in a sordid little inn at the shipping company's expense. While I was in this pickle, Soustelle arrived as General de Gaulle's emissary to rally the French colony. I was able to persuade my keepers to take me to him. He very politely explained to the Americans that I was not a spy. I waited in peace until I received the necessary documents and left for New York on a regular ship.

D.E. In a text reprinted in *The View from Afar,* you describe your move to New York.[1]

C.L.-S. I lived in a studio in Greenwich Village, on Eleventh Street, close to the corner of Sixth Avenue. Much later I learned that Claude Shannon, the founder of cybernetics, was also living in the building at the time.

---

1. "New York post et préfiguratif," in *Le Regard éloigné* (Paris: Plon, 1983); in English as "New York in 1941," in *The View from Afar,* trans. Joachim Neugroschel and Phoebe Hoss (New York: Basic Books, 1985).

D.E. And you never met him?

C.L.-S. Never. A young Belgian woman, who also lived in this red-brick apartment building—which was still standing in 1972 when I went to see it—told me one day that one of our neighbors "was inventing an artificial brain." Many years later I learned it was Shannon.

D.E. It's truly a shame that you never met him.

C.L.-S. It is too bad, but at the time I wouldn't have understood.

D.E. Did your English improve? To teach. . . .

C.L.-S. No. It was still rudimentary, but I arrived in the spring and classes were already over. I went to introduce myself at the New School where I was told all of a sudden, "You can't possibly call yourself Lévi-Strauss. Here you'll say your name is Claude L. Strauss." I asked why, and they said, "The students would find it funny." Because of the blue jeans! So for several years I lived in the States with a mutilated last name.

Ever since, this unfortunate coincidence has continued to haunt me. Like a ghost! Hardly a year goes by without my receiving, usually from Africa, an order for jeans. Shortly after 1950, in Paris, a total stranger came to my door, saying he sold fabric. He had found my name in the telephone book and wanted to propose my name for a pants factory. I objected, saying that my position at the university and as a scholar was incompatible with that sort of undertaking. He told me not to worry and explained that the affair would never see the light of day, all he would have to do was suggest it. "Rather than lose exclusive rights to their brand-name, the company would pay us handsomely to halt the project. All we would have to do is split the proceeds." I politely declined.

A few years ago I was at Berkeley as a visiting professor. One evening my wife and I wanted to have dinner in a restaurant where we didn't have reservations. There was a line. A waiter asked for our name so he could call us when our turn came. The moment he heard it, he asked, "The pants or the books?"

One has to admire the level of education of the waiters in California, for in Paris, when my wife leaves her name in a store for an order and people exclaim because it is such a well-known name, it's always because of the pants, never the books.

D.E. And after your change of identity?

C.L.-S. I was sent off with a monthly stipend. And I spent the summer writing *Family and Social Life of the Nambikwara* in English to learn the language.[2]

D.E. It wasn't published right away.

C.L.-S. No. It came out in France in 1948. It was my "complementary thesis."[3]

D.E. Once you arrived, you got to know the surrealists in exile in New York.

C.L.-S. Breton and I kept up our friendship. He introduced me to his old circle.

D.E. You were a young, unknown university professor, and you became part of a group of famous artists—stars, even—Breton, Tanguy, Duchamp. . . .

C.L.-S. And Leonora Carrington, Max Ernst, Dorothea Tanning, Matta, Wifredo Lam. . . . Masson and Calder were living in the country. I went to see them on a few weekends.

D.E. Did you like the members of the group?

C.L.-S. Some of them. I liked Max Ernst right away, and he is the one I stayed closest to. Tanguy, whose painting I admired a great deal, was not an easy person. Duchamp had great kindness, and for awhile Masson and I were very close. I also became friends with Patrick Waldberg. Our friendship continued after the war ended.

D.E. Peggy Guggenheim was financing the existence of the group?

C.L.-S. She helped this or that one out financially, but Max Ernst, whom she married, was more affluent than the others. They were leading the Bohemian life in Greenwich Village. Until Max Ernst left Peggy Guggenheim. One day, Breton called to ask me if I had a small sum of money to buy back one of his Indian objects from Max Ernst, who was now broke. This historic object is now in the Musée de l'Homme.

D.E. This little world had its social side, too?

2. "La Vie familiale et sociale des Indiens Nambikwara," in *Journal de la Société des Américanistes* (1948).

3. One of the requirements, along with a principal thesis, for the Franch academic degree *doctorat d'état.*—TRANS.

C.L.-S. We saw one another at various people's homes. The "truth game" was very fashionable.[4] And we would go out to sample the exotic restaurants of New York.

D.E. Playing the "truth game" with people like that must not have been easy!

C.L.-S. There was a lot of consideration for outsiders: myself, Pierre Lazareff, who sometimes came, also Denis de Rougemont.

D.E. How did you meet Lazareff?

C.L.-S. Breton, Duthuit, and I needed extra money and were working for the radio service directed by Lazareff at the OWI, the Office of War Information, on broadcasts for France. There we all were, among people from different backgrounds, and sometimes we would get together outside of work. There I became friends with Dolores Vanetti, with whom Sartre was later to fall in love.

D.E. Describe your radio work.

C.L.-S. I'd already had some experience with radio. To be less of a burden to my parents, I found a job as a student reading the bulletin for the Bureau International du Travail over the microphone at Radio Tour Eiffel in the basement of the Grand Palais. This was why my father painted me as a speaker when he made the huge (30 x 5 m.) murals for the Madagascar Pavillion (a country where he'd never set foot) for the Colonial Exposition.

Two or three times a week in New York, André Breton, Georges Duthuit, Robert Lebel, and I would read the news and propaganda texts issued by Lazareff's offices. I was given Roosevelt's speeches to read because it seemed that my voice could be heard best over the jamming.

D.E. How did you happen to find the work?

C.L.-S. Through Patrick Waldberg, whom I've already mentioned. He worked there too. He was both a poet and art critic. Later he wrote about Max Ernst and published some charming books on the turn of the century epoch. At the time we never would have guessed that back in Paris he would become a corresponding member of the Institut de France! He used to drink and lead a wild life, going to little bars in Harlem where he would sometimes bring me along.

---

4. A kind of psychoanalytic parlor game, of which André Breton was said to be particularly fond, the object of which was to elicit the participants' intimate feelings. Peggy Guggenheim mentions it in her memoir *Out of This Century: Confessions of an Art Addict* (New York: Universe Books, 1979).—TRANS.

D.E. If I'm to believe your essay on New York, one of your main activities at this time was acquiring artwork.

C.L.-S. Max Ernst had a passion for primitive art. On Third Avenue—which was very different from what it is now—he discovered a little German antique dealer who sold him an Indian artefact. At that time you almost never saw such things for sale. Max Ernst told us about the dealer. We had very little money, and whoever had a few dollars would purchase the coveted object. When Ernst was broke, he would let the others know. Since our antique dealer had found an outlet, more and more objects became available. In fact—I can tell the story now because it has been published—they came from a major museum that was selling them because they were considered duplicates of works in their collection. As if there could be duplicates! When the dealer discovered he had a market, he became the intermediary between the museum and ourselves.

D.E. Did you know that at the time?

C.L.-S. We very soon found out. With the help of the guard, he took us into the museum storehouses, in an isolated building in the New York suburbs. We would make our selection, and a few days later the objects would appear in his shop.

D.E. What became of the things you bought?

C.L.-S. I brought them back with me to France. But I had personal problems and had to sell them at Drouot's in 1951. The Musée de l'Homme and the museum in Leiden bought several of them. Also, private individuals, such as Lacan and, I believe, Malraux, bought a few others. I have two or three of them.

D.E. Did you maintain your ties with the surrealists after the war?

C.L.-S. With Ernst, Breton, and Waldberg, yes. I lost track of the others.

André Breton went back to France before I did, since in 1945 I was sent back to New York as the cultural counsellor to the French embassy. So we didn't see one another for three years. We had a ritual of going to the flea market every Saturday with his small band of followers. It was considered a great honor to be allowed to accompany Breton on this occasion.

D.E. Were you ever banished from the realm?

C.L.-S. Of course we had a row, for which I was unwittingly responsible. Breton had been asked to do a book that was to be called

L'Art magique. Inspiration failed him, and as one often does at such a pass, he made up a questionnaire, which he sent to me and some other people. I admired Breton. When we looked at art he had an infallible eye for objects, he was always right on the nose, never hesitating in his assessment. But the term "magic" had a precise meaning for me, it was part of the anthropological vocabulary. I didn't like to see it put to dubious uses. Instead of stating my objections, I preferred simply not to answer. Breton sent me another questionnaire. I was in the Cévennes on vacation with my son from my second marriage, who was seven at the time. The questionnaire came with reproductions of artworks you were supposed to rank as "more or less magical." Even if I objected to the project, I thought it would be interesting to have a child's reaction, and I thought it would interest Breton in the same way. Particularly since my son ranked the pictures without any hesitation. I sent it to Breton, who responded with an acerbic letter. The book came out, with my son's answers included. But the copy he sent to me bore a curt dedication to my son.

D.E.   And you didn't see one another again?

C.L.-S.   We more or less reconciled our differences, but it wasn't the same.

D.E.   And with Max Ernst?

C.L.-S.   Our friendship continued after New York. There was never a problem. When the Collège de France invited me to give the lectures for the Loubat Foundation—I was not yet a member, it was about the time I was turned down—Max Ernst came to hear me. I happened to describe a Hopi divinity while expressing my regret that I was unable to obtain a slide to illustrate my point. The following week, Max Ernst brought me a drawing big enough to show for a lecture. I still have it. Max Ernst's attitude toward anthropology was the opposite of Breton's. Breton distrusted it, he didn't like having scholarly matters get between him and the object. Max Ernst collected objects but also wanted to know everything about them.

D.E.   Did this contact with the surrealists influence you? I mean, in your work? Rodney Needham, in an article in *The Times Literary Supplement* in 1984, compares your work to that of the surrealists.

C.L.-S.   In a way, the comparison is valid. It is true that the surrealists and I all belong to an intellectual tradition that goes back to the second half of the nineteenth century. Breton had a passion for Gustave

Moreau, for the whole symbolist and neosymbolist period. The surrealists were attuned to the irrational and sought to exploit it from an aesthetic standpoint. This is part of the same material I work with, but I am guided by the intention of analyzing and understanding it while remaining sensitive to its beauty.

I will add that among this group there was a climate of intellectual ferment that did a great deal for me. Contact with the surrealists enriched and honed my aesthetic tastes. Many objects I would have rejected as unworthy appeared in a different light thanks to Breton and his friends.

D.E. You say in *The View from Afar* that the books in your Mythology series are put together like Max Ernst's collages!

C.L.-S. The surrealists taught me not to fear the abrupt and unexpected comparisons that Max Ernst liked to use in his collages. This influence can be seen in *The Savage Mind*. Max Ernst built personal myths out of images borrowed from another culture, I mean from old nineteenth-century books, and he made these images say more than they did when viewed by an innocent eye. In the Mythology books I also cut up a mythical subject and recombined the fragments to bring out more meaning.

*

D.E. September came, and you began teaching at the New School.

C.L.-S. During the summer I had made a few contacts with my American colleagues. Métraux, of course, from the time I arrived; Lowie, to whom in large part I owed my invitation. He was living in Berkeley but came to New York from time to time. I had gone to introduce myself to Boas who, as is the custom for retired American professors (and Boas had retired some thirty years before), still kept his office at Columbia.

D.E. You and Métraux got on well together.

C.L.-S. Yes, he became a close friend.

D.E. When did you meet him?

C.L.-S. After getting back from my expedition among the Nambikwara. I was about to return to France. Métraux, with whom I'd carried on a sporadic correspondence, told me that on the way back from Argentina he would be stopping for a few hours in Santos—

that's the port for Saõ Paulo—and that we could finally meet. For half a day we walked along deserted beaches with the memory of sixteenth-century voyagers hovering over us.

D.E. He was living in New York?

C.L.-S. Washington. But he often came to New York. Then he would spend the night at my place. We'd divide up the bedding.

D.E. Was he a friendly person?

C.L.-S. Very much so. And also profoundly neurotic, going from euphoria to a state of the deepest depression. He was also a glutton for work—if he wasn't writing all the time he was miserable.

D.E. What was his position?

C.L.-S. He worked for the Bureau of American Ethnology, where the effort to compile the *Handbook of South American Indians* was underway. I was asked at once to participate in the project.

D.E. Did he have an influence on your work?

C.L.-S. Not on my work. Alfred Métraux was not a theoretician but a great scholar and fieldworker, which did not keep him from having a very lively intellectual curiosity in other realms. He provided me with an enormous amount of information. He himself had been involved with the surrealists at an earlier date. He was close to Bataille and Leiris. Later, in Paris, we saw each other all the time. That went on until his death. It overwhelmed me as it did all his friends. But now, when I think back on it, it seems to me that his private life was a long preparation for suicide.

D.E. You were saying that you had gone to see Franz Boas.

C.L.-S. The moment I got to New York, I asked to see him. He was the great man of American anthropology and had enormous prestige. He was one of these nineteenth-century titans, the likes of which are no more to be found, whose output demanded respect not only for its quantity but its diversity: physical anthropology, linguistics, ethnography, archeology, mythology, folklore, nothing was foreign to him. His work covers the entirety of the anthropological domain. All of American anthropology issued from him.

D.E. He had taken part in the rescue of European scholars and artists; Jimmy Ernst, Max Ernst's son, tells in his book that it was Boas who made it possible for them to come to the United States.[5]

5. Jimmy Ernst, *L'Ecart absolu* (Paris: Balland, 1987).

C.L.-S. Boas's life was not without its problems. When the First World War broke out, he remained a German at heart and fought against America's entry into the conflict. After the war, this position earned him the hostility of many of his colleagues. During the Second World War, when he was already quite elderly and had been retired for a long time, his authority was of the moral type. He acted personally on behalf of former compatriots. And of course, he was one of the very first and most acute opponents of racist ideas, so what was happening in his native country pained him a great deal.

D.E. Had you read all his works when you arrived in the United States?

C.L.-S. I hadn't read them all, but I knew of some of them. Boas welcomed me kindly, nothing more. I was obviously unknown to him.

But I saw him later on. First with Jakobson, for they had many linguistic interests in common and often discussed them. Boas invited us once to dinner at his house in Grantwood, across the Hudson. In his dining room was a superb carved and painted chest made by the Kwakiutl Indians, the subject of a large part of his work. I admired the piece and said thoughtlessly that living with Indians capable of creating such masterpieces must have been a unique experience. He answered drily, "They are Indians like any others." I imagine that his cultural relativism didn't permit him to establish a hierarchy of values among peoples. He had a very strict intellectual puritanism.

A few weeks later, Dr. Rivet, who had taken refuge in Colombia, came through New York before going to Mexico. Boas held a luncheon in his honor.

D.E. Was Rivet still director of the Musée de l'Homme?

C.L.-S. Yes, he had been a professor at the museum since 1928, and he had transformed the Musée d'Ethnographie of the Trocadéro into the Musée de l'Homme, housed in the Palais de Chaillot, which had been built for the Exposition Universelle in 1937. He had to flee once the Germans had overpowered the resistance network at the Musée de l'Homme. Several of his collaborators were executed or deported. He himself barely escaped.

The luncheon was held at the Columbia Faculty Club. It was during the winter, which was incredibly cold. Boas arrived wearing an old fur hat that must have dated from his expeditions among the Eskimos sixty years earlier. His daughter Mrs. Yampolski and several of his colleagues from Columbia were there, all former students: Ruth Benedict, Ralph Linton, and a few others. Boas was very jovial. In the middle of a conversation, he shoved himself violently away from the table and fell backwards. I was seated next to him and bent down to lift him up. Rivet, who had started his career as a military doctor, tried in vain to revive him. Boas was dead.

D.E. Did his work mean a great deal to you?

C.L.-S. It was essential. I was always interested in the Indians of the Northwest coast, and he had written a great deal about them. Today it has become fashionable to criticize him for his unsystematic approach, his aversion to theory, and the disorganized character of his work. But Boas was faced with a prodigious mass of material, which he gathered or had literate natives collect for him. He received texts written in several Indian languages and translated it all himself! He is also criticized for having adopted a variety of positions, depending on the subject matter on which he was working.

It seems to me that on the contrary the diversity of Boas's interests led to the richness of American anthropology during its best period: from Lowie's critical empiricism to Ruth Benedict's patterns of culture, or the attention Margaret Mead paid to individual psychology in its relationship to culture. All of this was already in Boas. In the generation or, rather, the generations that he taught, each was able to draw on one aspect of his teaching or work and develop it. Except for Kroeber, who tried to keep all the aspects together.

D.E. Meeting such a man must have been enormously exciting for you, as you were still in the formative years of your career.

C.L.-S. Boas is responsible for certain basic ideas. For example, he is the one who proved, in his work in physical anthropology, that the cephalic index, considered by anthropologists as an invariable trait that could be utilized to define the races, was a function of environmental influences. By studying successive generations of immigrants to the United States, he established that anatomical differences once clearly visible between ethnic groups gradually diminished. Likewise concerning the differential rhythm of the growth rates of children. The criticism of racism begins with Boas.

His linguistic work was also immense. He alone probably wrote more grammars of indigenous languages—about a dozen—than any other linguist who ever lived. It is because of him that we now understand that it is pointless to wish to reduce the grammar of exotic languages to Indo-European models.

Boas was also one of the first—somewhere I wrote that it was Saussure, but in fact Saussure never expressed himself on the subject, it flows indirectly from his work—to insist on an essential fact in the human sciences: the laws of language function on an unconscious level, beyond the control of speaking subjects; thus they can be studied as objective phenomena, representative for this reason of other social facts. Boas stated this fundamental principal in 1911 in his justifiably famous preface to the *Handbook of American Indian Languages*.

Finally, in the area of folklore and mythology, he accumulated a fantastic store of material that for preposterous reasons has been the object of scorn. For example, Boas encouraged one of his informants to write down all of his tribe's recipes for food, and he translated and published them with the idea that it is impossible to predict what will be important and what will not. In the study of a little-known or unknown culture, apparently insignificant details are sometimes the most revealing.

This minutiae has been ridiculed. However, the Kwakiutl recipes gave me the key to certain mythological problems by revealing relationships of compatibility and incompatibility among foods, relationships that are not solely a question of taste.

True, Boas's work is not easy to use. One has to take the trouble. But it is of extraordinary richness.

D.E. Between 1941 and 1944, you spent time with the whole American anthropological circle.

C.L.-S. Yes. So I knew Ralph Linton and Ruth Benedict well. Each one used to invite me to dinner to criticize the other. It was the talk of Columbia; they hated one another.

D.E. And Kroeber?

C.L.-S. Like Lowie, he lived in California and from time to time came to New York. Something strange: I was present at Boas's death and came close to being there for Kroeber's. He was passing through Paris with his wife, and the two were to come to my house for dinner. That very morning, Mrs. Kroeber telephoned to tell me her husband had died during the night. She didn't know anyone in Paris. I went to their hotel on the Quai Voltaire to help her.

D.E. The American school of anthropology was particularly active.

C.L.-S. Like the English school. But the United States is an immense country, and consequently there were many anthropologists, just as there were quantities of everything else.

D.E. Let's get back to the autumn of 1941: you began your courses at the New School.

C.L.-S. I had been asked—it was the beginning of the Good Neighbor Policy—to give a course on contemporary Latin American sociology. Other than Brazil, I knew nothing at all. So every day I went to the New York Public Library to teach myself about the social realities and political life of Argentina, Peru, and other countries.

D.E. Who came to hear you?

C.L.-S. The same as for my colleagues—courses were attended in part by refugees who spoke English no better than we did, and New Yorkers who came there for instruction. It was a good deal like an "open" university. I taught for several years, always contemporary Latin America. During the winter of 1941–42 the Ecole libre des Hautes Etudes de New York was founded. I taught there in French, ethnological subjects that I was free to choose.

D.E. So you had two teaching jobs at once.

C.L.-S. That's right.

D.E. How did the Ecole come to be founded?

C.L.-S. I believe that Boris Mirkine-Guetzévitch had the initial idea. He was a jurist of Russian origin who it appears had played a role on the liberal side in the beginning of the Russian revolution. He quickly left Russia for France, where he became naturalized. His daughter, Vitia Hessel, with whom I was a good friend in New York, was a writer. She died only recently. *Les Temps modernes* just published a short story of hers.

Mirkine-Guetzévitch had a fertile mind. He loved to dream up and found all kinds of organizations under the auspices of some celebrity. He would keep the vice presidency but remain in charge. He knew better than anyone how to obtain backing. English has a word for this type of person, "go-between," which is untranslatable because it has two levels of meaning—complementary but also somewhat ironic. Mirkine-Guetzévitch rallied support for his project from famous people: Jacques Maritain, Henri Focillon, Jean Perrin, the Belgian Byzantinist Henri Grégoire, I forget the rest.

D.E. Where did he get the funding?

C.L.-S. The money came from several patrons and Free France. The Americans helped solve administrative and practical problems.

D.E. Where was the Ecole?

C.L.-S. Right next to the New School, on Fifth Avenue, almost at the corner of Twelfth Street.

D.E. And you were asked to participate right away?

C.L.-S. By Mirkine-Guetzévitch, who wanted me to be the general secretary of the new institution. But Alexandre Koyré wanted the position. We were on good terms, and I went along.

D.E. And it was Koyré, I believe, who introduced you to Jakobson, who also had been asked to teach there.

C.L.-S. He had the feeling that Jakobson and I shared certain qualities of mind.

D.E. This meeting was a decisive one for you?

C.L.-S. It was enormously important. At the time I was a kind of naive structuralist, a structuralist without knowing it. Jakobson revealed to me the existence of a body of doctrine that had already been formed within a discipline, linguistics, with which I was unacquainted. For me it was a revelation.

D.E. . . . and the beginning of a great friendship.

C.L.-S. Both at once. From the first we felt close intellectually, destined to become friends. Was there some misunderstanding at the start? Jakobson has said that when he met me he said to himself, "At last, someone I can drink all night with!" Now I have no stomach for alcohol, and I don't like to go to bed late. Whatever the case, it was the beginning of a brotherly friendship, even though he was twelve years older than I.

D.E. A friendship that never failed.

C.L.-S. A friendship of forty years without a break. It is a bond that never weakened, and, for me, an admiration that never ended.

A few days before he died, I received an offprint from him inscribed, "To my brother Claude."

D.E. What kind of man was he?

C.L.-S. He was a thinker of an intellectual power that dominated all around him. He mastered a number of languages; his erudition was prodigious, ranging from the linguists of ancient India up to Husserl. . . . He was interested in everything—painting, avant-garde poetry, anthropology, computers, biology. . . .

D.E. He had been an ethnologist in his youth.

C.L.-S. He had begun his career, still almost a teenager, making surveys of folklore in the Moscow area with Bogatyrev, the great Russian ethnologist. He also took part in the modernist movement of Russian painters and poets.

D.E. You saw him a great deal afterward in Paris.

C.L.-S. Regularly, when he came to France, and he traveled a lot! During the fifties, my third wife, Monique, and I lived in a little apartment where the Rue St. Lazare begins, near the church of Notre-Dame-de-Lorette. There was not enough room to put him up so we would rent him a room in a hotel nearby. Each of his visits gave us great pleasure and inspired some fear as well, for we didn't have his physical stamina or intellectual vitality. He would ring at eight in the morning for breakfast, spend the day with us, and sometimes stay far into the night to talk.

Things worked out later on. I introduced him to Lacan, who was a good friend of mine. As could be expected, Lacan was immediately taken with him, and so was his wife, Sylvia. They each had an apartment in adjoining buildings on Rue de Lille and welcomed my suggestion to invite Jakobson to stay when he came to Paris. So for several years Jakobson had "his room" at Sylvia Lacan's.

D.E. In New York he also taught at the Ecole libre.

C.L.-S. His courses were stunning. He spoke French with ease, almost without notes. He would take a small packet of notes out of his pocket and look at it from time to time. Above all, his dramatic gift was unequalled; he transported his audience, who had the justifiable impression that they were experiencing a key moment in the history of thought.

D.E. What were his courses about?

C.L.-S. His courses came out a few years ago, under the title, *Six Lectures on Sound and Meaning.*[6] Upon his request, since I had heard them, I wrote the preface.

D.E. Did he attend your courses?

C.L.-S. I was giving a course on kinship. Jakobson came to my course and I went to his. He told me one day that I should write about

---

6. Roman Jakobson, *Six Leçons sur le son et le sens,* preface by Claude Lévi-Strauss (Paris: Minuit, 1976); English edition, *Six Lectures on Sound and Meaning,* trans. John Mepham (Cambridge: MIT Press, 1978).

it. I had never thought about it, and it was because of his encouragement that in 1943 I began writing *Elementary Structures of Kinship*.[7] I
finished it in 1947.

*

D.E. You were teaching, writing . . . What were your days like?

C.L.-S. Every morning I went to the New York Public Library.
What I know of anthropology I learned during those years. I was
there when it opened and didn't leave until around twelve or one
o'clock. I would eat in a food shop and then go home to write.

D.E. The New York Public Library must be a spectacular place.

C.L.-S. There were a lot of people there, but few from the
university—they preferred the Columbia library. I preferred Forty-
second Street because it was closer to my place. It had a great attraction for me. It was a little antiquated, as is often the case with old
New York institutions, but full of charm.

D.E. Nevertheless there was an important ethnological collection
there?

C.L.-S. It was considerable. Even this library, which was meant
for the general public, had a very rich collection that was kept up-to-
date. There I found a large part of the source materials I used in *Elementary Structures of Kinship*.

D.E. That is one of the objections often made against you: you
have read a great deal but have done little fieldwork.

C.L.-S. That was the result of circumstances. If I had gotten a visa
for Brazil in 1940, I would have gone back to my initial fieldsites and
done more work. If the war hadn't broken out, I would probably have
gone on another mission. Fate led me to the United States, where due
to a lack of means and the international situation I was not in a position to launch any expeditions but where, on the other hand, I was
entirely free to work on theoretical issues. In that respect, I can say,
the possibilities were limitless.

I also became aware that in the previous twenty or thirty years a
considerable quantity of material had been accumulated; but it was in

7. Claude Lévi-Strauss, *Les Structures élémentaires de la parenté* (Paris: Presses Universitaires de France, 1949; 2d ed., The Hague: Mouton, 1967); English edition, *The Elementary Structures of Kinship* (Boston: Beacon Press, 1969).

such disarray that one didn't know where to begin or how to utilize it. It seemed urgent to sort out what this mass of documents had brought us. Finally, why not admit it? I realized early on that I was a library man, not a fieldworker. I don't mean this disparagingly, quite the contrary, but fieldwork is a kind of "women's work" (which is probably why women are so successful at it). Myself, I had neither the interest nor the patience for it.

D.E. However, despite the dangers that we have already mentioned, you seemed to take a great deal of pleasure from it.

C.L.-S. Indeed. But these were my first trips. I'm not sure that, had there been others, I wouldn't have felt a growing exasperation when faced with the disproportion between usable time and time wasted.

This was true at the time of my fieldwork, and things have only gotten worse. A few days ago I received from Canada, as a curiosity, the questionnaires, forms, and other papers that must now be filled out in multiple copies before a "band" (that is the official term) of Indians in British Columbia will grant anyone permission to do fieldwork. They will not tell you a myth unless the informant receives written assurance that he retains literary ownership, with all the legal consequences it entails. You must admit that this meddlesome bureaucracy, this mania for paperwork—a caricature of our own customs— has eliminated much of the old attraction of fieldwork!

D.E. Did you ever have the same feelings Malinowski described in his diary? These feelings of irritation, even disgust?

C.L.-S. Absolutely. When the diary first came out, some anthropologists had the hypocrisy to be indignant, claiming that it put Malinowski's work in a bad light. But who hasn't had such moments of depression? Métraux, who did an enormous amount of fieldwork, would discuss them willingly. You know, when you have spent two weeks with a native group without being able to get anything out of the people around you simply because you annoy them, you begin to hate them.

D.E. Did this happen to you?

C.L.-S. In the unforgiving landscape of central Brazil, there was many a time I had the feeling I was wasting my life! To get back to what you were saying a minute ago and without comparing myself to Malinowski, I did more fieldwork than my critics would admit. In any case, I did enough to learn and to understand what fieldwork is, which is an essential prerequisite for making a sound evaluation and use of the work done by others. Let's say that my field experiences represented what psychoanalysts call a "didactic." At the same time I believe I made a few finds and brought back some new data.

*

D.E. When you were in New York did you pursue your political interests? For example, did you spend any time in Gaullist circles?

C.L.-S. I had signed on with the Free French Forces. I was assigned to what was called the French Scientific Mission in the United States. Soustelle, on his way through New York, insisted in a friendly way that I follow him to London. But I wanted to study, and soon I wanted to write. I attended a few Gaullist meetings, but I was not very active.

D.E. It was at this time that your political involvement came to an end?

C.L.-S. I would say it faded away.

D.E. And then one fine day you heard of the Normandy invasion?

C.L.-S. I remember the day. I was in my studio in Greenwich Village, getting up in the morning. I had turned on my little radio to listen to the news. What I was hearing was so strange that at first it was unintelligible. Little by little I understood and I burst into sobs.

D.E. After the Liberation, you requested your repatriation to France?

C.L.-S. Things didn't go exactly that way. Koyré had resigned from his position as general secretary of the Ecole libre. There had been some conflict. Two types of attitudes came to light among the professors, whose numbers had substantially increased. Those who considered themselves wholly French had only one idea, to return to France and take up their profession. In their eyes, after the war the Ecole would have no reason to exist and should be discontinued. Other colleagues, recently naturalized or foreigners who had found refuge in France before the war, were unsure of the fate awaiting them. They wondered what was going to happen in France and preferred to wait and see; they wished to maintain the Ecole, which kept up their tie with France while permitting them to stay in the shelter of the United States. Koyré ardently felt himself to be French, but he disliked taking sides. I succeeded him as the representative of the first group.

In France they were aware of the problem, for Henri Laugier, appointed director of cultural relations, had himself been a refugee in Canada. He called me to try to find a solution. So I returned to Paris after a difficult voyage in an American naval convoy (the war was still on). We landed at an English port—I don't know which one. I went to London, where V-2 rockets were falling, then to Dieppe, and from there to Paris, in an American truck. It was early January 1945. I occupied a small office at the directory of cultural relations, which had moved into a hotel—not a private hotel, but an old furnished hotel—on Rue Lord Byron near the Champs-Elysées.

D.E. What was your title?

C.L.-S. My only title was that of secretary general of the Ecole Libre des hautes études de New York.

D.E. But what did you do?

C.L.-S. I was responsible for meeting with people who wished to visit the United States. I have only two distinct recollections. There I became reacquainted with Merleau-Ponty, who was among those wishing to go to the United States.

D.E. You hadn't seen one another since your probation for the *agrégation?*

C.L.-S. This was the first time.

D.E. How did the meeting go?

C.L.-S. It went very well. Since I knew nothing or almost nothing of what was going on in France, I asked him what existentialism was. He answered: an attempt to reestablish great philosophy in the tradition of Descartes and Kant.

D.E. And you had a discussion with him on the subject.

C.L.-S. I wasn't up-to-date. I hadn't even read *Being and Nothingness.*

D.E. And your second memory?

C.L.-S. Jeanine Micheau, who was a famous singer at the time, came to see me. She walked into my office, heavily perfumed, leading two enormous dogs on leashes.

4

Back to the Old World

D.E. You were only in Paris for a few months, and then you went back to New York.

C.L.-S. . . . as cultural counsellor to the French embassy. Laugier wanted to appoint me to Mexico. But I was writing *Elementary Structures of Kinship,* and I needed the American libraries. I insisted that he allow me to succeed Henri Seyrig, who was a close friend of mine. Seyrig was for the idea as well.

D.E. The father of the actress?

C.L.-S. Yes, Delphine's father. I used to see her as a little girl at her parents' place. Seyrig was an archeologist of some repute (later he was appointed director of the French museums). Our joint effort convinced Laugier to give me the job.

D.E. When did you get back to New York?

C.L.-S. In the spring of 1945.

D.E. What were your duties?

C.L.-S. Basically, it was to remodel a building!

D.E. The present one?

C.L.-S. No, the present building of the consul general. Just before the war, the French government had acquired a splendid mansion on Fifth Avenue built for an American banker in the style of a Roman palace. The mayor of New York, who was strongly anti-Vichy, had prevented the representatives of the Vichy government from occupying it. When de Gaulle came to power, the mayor finally gave permission to move in. The building was hardly appropriate for the needs of the cultural services. I was given the task of refitting it. Jacques Carlu, the architect who designed the Palais de Chaillot and who was a refugee in the United States, was willing to help me. We redid the whole interior.

D.E. It must have been an enormous job.

C.L.-S. Yes, but it's work I enjoy. Much more than the job of cultural counsellor. Trying out ideas, drawing plans, being part of the
life on a construction job, sometimes even getting to do some of the
work, all that delights me.

D.E. But you also had to carry out the functions of cultural counsellor!

C.L.-S. Indeed I was supposed to! But I enjoyed some leeway, because during the construction the whole service was camping out in
what had been the grand salon—a ballroom, to be truthful.

D.E. And did you see your friends again in New York?

C.L.-S. The emigré circles were beginning to disperse. I had been
involved in a number of them, which had only partially overlapped:
the surrealists, the university community—the psychoanalysts, as
well, for at Raymond de Saussure's (son of the great linguist) I would
often see Loewenstein, Kris, Nunberg, and, once, even Marie Bonaparte. My functions as cultural counsellor brought me into a different group, wealthy Americans friendly to France. A different New
York was revealed to me.

D.E. You stayed for three years.

C.L.-S. I returned to Paris at the end of 1947.

D.E. While you were cultural counsellor, Sartre made a visit to the
United States.

C.L.-S. Yes, but he didn't need me to organize his stay. We had
lunch once, the two of us.

D.E. You didn't know him?

C.L.-S. Not at all. I had seen him when I was getting ready for the *agrégation,* for I was taking classes at the Ecole Normale Supérieure.
Someone pointed him out to me, saying. "That's Sartre." Already it
was important to know who Sartre was!

D.E. You also saw Simone de Beauvoir in New York.

C.L.-S. She came on her own, somewhat later. But she didn't need
the cultural services of the embassy, either. Since I knew her a little,
we reestablished contact. I invited her to lunch at my home. I remember it very well—my son had just been born—she looked at the crib
with such revulsion! A baby was not the thing to show her!

D.E. And I believe that you entertained Camus?

C.L.-S. He had more need of the cultural services. I took him for a
walk around town, to dinner in Chinatown. . . . And we spent an

evening in a club on Lower Broadway where there was a comedy act featuring women singers past their prime. The female clown is a typically American genre one ought to know, but I've always found it distasteful.

D.E. Did you entertain other personalities?

C.L.-S. Jules Romains. But at the time, I still had principles. Just before the war he had published a questionable book, not at all like *Les Hommes de bonne volonté,* which I had read avidly. Furthermore, Jules Romains had been invited not by the cultural services of the embassy but by certain Franco-American organizations whose positions during the war had been rather ambiguous. They invited me to give a talk during which I said some disagreeable things to Jules Romains. I praised *Les Hommes de bonne volonté* and recalled that my generation still felt an affinity toward the two heroes of the book, Jallez and Jerphanion, who had promised each other never to enter the Académie française—which had just elected Jules Romains. André Maurois, who attended the meeting, mentions the stinging remarks of the cultural counsellor.

I also received a mission of young doctors that included M. Yves Laporte, today the administrator of the Collège de France. I hosted Jean Delay, who became my colleague at the Académie. And Gaston Berger, who would later become director of higher education.

D.E. And the father of Maurice Béjart.

C.L.-S. Yes. In those days I believe he was teaching in Aix. When he arrived, I was packing. I apologized for being such a poor host and explained that I was about to leave. He answered, "I know. You are going to the Collège." As I have already said, I hardly knew what the Collège de France was: a fearsome place, off limits, where as a student I didn't allow myself to enter. So I paid no attention to Gaston Berger's remark. When I arrived in Paris, Laugier, who was fond of me, told me that Henri Piéron wished to see me. You know who he was—the famous psychologist, communist, professor at the Collège de France. I made an appointment with him. He told me, "We intend to have you enter the Collège." I didn't know who "we" were, but he seemed quite sure of himself, and I thought that everything was arranged by mysterious powers, that all I needed to do was let myself be carried along. I had lived outside of France for the past thirteen years and was in no position to understand that I was going to be the stakes in a battle between clans inside the Collège, between liberals and conservatives. I was defeated. Inconceivably, when one knows the ways of the Collège, I was persuaded to stand again a few months later when another chair fell vacant, and again I was defeated.

D.E. When did this double misfortune take place?

C.L.-S. In 1949 and 1950.

D.E. That was when Dumézil was elected. Against the wishes of the administrator, Edmond Faral.

C.L.-S. Who had coldly warned me that I would never enter the Collège! The combined efforts of Dumézil, Bataillon, and Benveniste did not succeed in swaying the assembly. When speaking of Max Ernst before, I mentioned the Loubat lectures: ironically, at the same time, when I was about to be defeated, I was invited to give a series of lectures. Dumézil attended. That was when I really met him.

D.E. It took you ten years to present yourself again as a candidate, and this time it was a success.

C.L.-S. I had been the innocent, unwittingly brought into a quarrel between ancients and moderns: the traditionalists still included men who, by their spirit and arrogance, belonged to another century. I must say that as soon as Marcel Bataillon replaced Faral as administrator of the Collège, these conflicts began to abate. In my twenty-two years at the Collège, under the administration of Bataillon and his successors, I have never seen them reappear.

After this double disaster, I was convinced that I would never have a real career. I broke with my past, rebuilt my private life, and wrote *Tristes Tropiques,* which I would never have dared publish if I had been competing for a university position.

D.E. In New York you had put the finishing touches on *Elementary Structures of Kinship.*

C.L.-S. I had an arrangement with Louis Joxe, Laugier's successor at Cultural Relations. He allowed me to serve as counsellor half-time: mornings at the office, afternoons at my home to write. It is true that my second wife and I were living upstairs, in the penthouse of the building. In emergencies, I only had to come downstairs. In that way I was able to finish the book.

D.E. You presented it as a thesis once you came back to Paris.

C.L.-S. As the principal thesis. And *Family and Social Life of the Nambikwara* as the complementary thesis.

D.E. How was your jury formed?

C.L.-S. I went to see Davy, who was dean of the Sorbonne, with my manuscript under my arm, to ask him to be my thesis director (in a manner of speaking, since the thesis was already finished). He received me kindly, which was not his wont (he was of a cantankerous disposition). And he consented. The same thing for the complementary thesis, which Griaule accepted. So I defended at the Sorbonne with a jury composed of Davy, Griaule, Benveniste, Bayet, and Escarra, a sinologist interested in the law. That was in 1948.

D.E. Did you know Benveniste?

C.L.-S. Once I got back to France I went to see him as well as Dumézil. Jakobson had entrusted me with various errands for them. Since *Elementary Structures* covered the whole world, I needed someone on the jury for each major geographical area. For India, I suggested that Davy call on Benveniste.

D.E. You had ties with him afterward?

C.L.-S. We had a lengthy correspondence because of this defense and the objections he made. Then, but much later, when I entered the Collège, I got to know him better. Benveniste was very reserved and did not easily form attachments. Once I invited him to dinner at the house. It took vast storehouses of diplomacy to convince him to come. According to Jakobson, he had not always been so withdrawn. Something had changed since their youth, when, Jakobson said, Benveniste had been happy and spontaneous.

D.E. *Elementary Structures of Kinship* came out in 1949?

C.L.-S. Yes, published by Presses Universitaires de France.

D.E. But *Family and Social Life of the Nambikwara Indians* had already been published?

C.L.-S. It had appeared as a report of about one hundred pages in the *Journal de la Société des Américanistes*. It was published as an offprint for my thesis defense. *Elementary Structures* appeared shortly afterward. I defended from the typed manuscript.

D.E. And Simone de Beauvoir reviewed your book when it came out.

C.L.-S. She was finishing *The Second Sex*. Michel Leiris talked to me about it one day at the Musée de l'Homme. I told Leiris that I myself had just finished a work on close to the same subject. Leiris repeated it to Simone de Beauvoir, who came to read the proofs of *Elementary Structures* at my house because she wanted to know the

latest state of anthropological research before completing her book.
When the book appeared, she reviewed it in *Les Temps modernes*.[1]

D.E. It was a very flattering article.

C.L.-S. Even warm. Note that at the time *Les Temps modernes*
wanted to be at the center of intellectual life. They were ready to welcome me without troubling over whether I was an existentialist or
not.

D.E. What about the overall reception of the book?

C.L.-S. It was very well received in anthropological circles. But I
cannot say that outside of those professional circles the book aroused
much interest.

D.E. It must be said that it is extremely technical.

C.L.-S. Admittedly. Moreover, my idea was to write a second volume, which I had already begun to think about and which was to be
called *Les Structures de parenté complexes*.

D.E. You put it aside?

C.L.-S. I quickly realized that it was impossible to deal with these
complex systems in a makeshift fashion: it would take computers to
do the job. I didn't have the practical, or certainly the intellectual,
means to undertake the project.

D.E. *Elementary Structures* already contains a "mathematical ap-
pendix" written by André Weil.

C.L.-S. Historically speaking, these pages have a great importance.
The entire mathematics of kinship, which has developed a great deal
since then, came out of them. And has continued in that vein.

D.E. You met Andrè Weil, Simone's brother, in the United States?

C.L.-S. Simone Weil's brother and also one of the founders of the
Bourbaki group. I was working on problems of Australian kinship so
complex that I thought it would take a mathematician to solve them.
I looked up Hadamard, who was also a refugee in the United States—
he was already quite old, but a famous mathematician. I posed the
problem to him, and—I believe I've told the story elsewhere—he said
that mathematicians know only the four operations and marriage
could not be included among any of them. Still pursuing the matter I
met André Weil, another refugee. I told him about my visit to Hadamard. His reaction was completely different. There is no need,

---

1. *Les Temps modernes* 49 (November 1949).

he said, to define marriage from a mathematical standpoint. Only relations between marriages are of interest. I gave him the data for the problem, and he produced the analysis you just mentioned.

D.E. For you it was a way to establish the scientific basis for your work?

C.L.-S. This mathematical demonstration went further, but it was in line with what I was trying to work out on a more modest level for systems of less complexity. Above all, it proceeded from principles akin to those Jakobson applied in linguistics, since in both cases the focus moves from the terms themselves to the relationships operating between them. That was exactly what I was attempting to do to resolve the puzzles marriage rules posed to anthropologists.

*

D.E. We have spoken of your failures at the Collège de France. What were your university functions after you returned to France in 1948?

C.L.-S. For several months I was maître de recherche at the Centre National de la Recherche Scientifique. It was a transitional job. Then I was assistant director of the Musée de l'Homme.

D.E. Who brought you to the Musée de l'Homme?

C.L.-S. Dr. Rivet. Just before retiring, he appointed me as assistant director for ethnology. André Leroi-Gourhan, assistant director for prehistory, was teaching in Lyons and was not always at the museum. For a year, until Rivet's successor was chosen, I had to deal with most of the problems.

D.E. This was when you met Leiris, who also worked at the Musée de l'Homme.

C.L.-S. I didn't know his work and read it with delight. Monique, my wife (we were already living together and were married in 1954), knew the Leiris. I had met her at Lacan's.

D.E. How did you meet Lacan?

C.L.-S. Koyré got us together one evening. My friendship with Georges-Henri Rivière also dates from that time. He had a standing invitation for meals at our house and would come over when his bachelor's solitude weighed too heavily upon him.

D.E. It was at this time that you completely gave up your political activities?

C.L.-S. Completely.

D.E. Gaullism never exerted any pull?

C.L.-S. No. I was still too strongly imbued with socialism to make the move to Gaullism. And at the same time, each political position seemed contradictory to me. I had attained some distance during the years in Brazil. Not entirely by my doing, moreover. In the years before the *agrégation,* as you recall, I had been working with Georges Monnet, the socialist deputy. In 1936, I was already in Brazil, and he became minister in the government of the Popular Front. I was expecting him to call me. It was obvious that in their victory my former comrades had forgotten me. Events, the new course my life was taking, did the rest. . . .

D.E. But you continued to take an interest in political life?

C.L.-S. Of course, and I still do.

D.E. After your years at the Musée de l'Homme, you taught at the Ecole des hautes études.

C.L.-S. From the time of my return I taught at the Institut d'Ethnologie, which operated at the Musée de l'Homme. Then I was elected to the Ecole des hautes études, to the chair held by Maurice Leenhardt, who was retiring. He had no desire to see me as his successor: he supported one of his students. It was a delicate situation, for at the Ecole the wishes of the retiring professor are generally respected. However, I was selected, largely because of Dumézil's support. But since one does not apply for candidacy at the Ecole—one is named—I only learned of his role in the past few years.

D.E. You were in the Fifth Section, Religious Sciences?

C.L.-S. That's right.

D.E. It was located at the Sorbonne.

C.L.-S. It still is, at stairway E.

D.E. What were your courses about?

C.L.-S. The name of the chair was "Religions of Noncivilized Peoples," as in the days when Mauss held it. I had to change the name quickly, and here is the reason. One day I was talking about the customs of an African people, and a black listener I didn't know got up and said, "I belong to this society and don't agree with your interpretation." Two or three other incidents of the sort led me to change the name of the chair to "Religions of Nonliterate Peoples." You couldn't say that people who came to the Sorbonne to discuss with you were "noncivilized"! That they did not possess their own writing was a fact.

D.E. In *Paroles données,* where you gathered the summaries of your courses at the Ecole des hautes études and at the Collège de France, there is a footnote containing an odd story; you tell of a meeting in Paris in 1953 with Talcott Parsons, who not only proposed a job for you at Harvard but had the contract there all ready.[2]

C.L.-S. I had met Talcott Parsons at Harvard, where I gave a lecture while I was cultural counsellor . . .

D.E. And you kept in touch . . .

C.L.-S. Not at all. In fact, I was surprised that this famous sociologist proposed a meeting with me, particularly since he gave no reason. It turned out that the original idea had come from Clyde Kluckhohn, the Harvard anthropologist, with whom I had always gotten along.

I put the note in *Paroles données* for the sake of an American woman who had made the spiteful comment in a book that I had returned to France because I couldn't find a job in the United States. From the American standpoint, it was the only explanation for going back to Europe. The same misunderstanding occurred with Robert Redfield. We liked one another, I even stayed at his home. I referred to this visit without naming him in an article, "New York in 1941,"[3] where I describe the very picturesque pioneer house that an American sociologist still had in the Chicago suburbs. He encouraged me to stay in the United States, and as I turned a deaf ear, he told Métraux that I was "a case of European tiredness." In fact, I could have settled in the United States from early on. At the very beginning, Kurt Lewin had offered me a steady position; after my failures at the Collège, Kroeber also made me an offer. Now Parsons was offering me exceptional conditions. The contract made me full professor with tenure. But I had no desire to start life as an exile again.

On several occasions I had to decide whether to return to France or to remain in the United States, but such choices have had no bearing on the feelings of profound gratitude I have toward that country.

2. Claude Lévi-Strauss, *Paroles données* (Paris Plon, 1984), p. 258; English edition, *Anthropology and Myth,* trans. Roy Willis (Oxford: Basil Blackwell, 1987).

3. *The View from Afar,* p. 266.

The help I received there probably saved my life, and for several years I found there an intellectual climate and the opportunity for work that to a large extent have made me who I am. Only, I knew in my bones that I belonged to the Old World, irrevocably.

D.E. However, professionally, you must be defined as an Americanist!

C.L.-S. That happened by chance. My first overseas post happened to be in Brazil. At the time I had the vaguest of notions about South America. In fact, I would have gone anywhere.

Ask me instead why I remained an Americanist. First, it seems to me, because of the unforgettable impression provoked by contact with the New World, where everything is on an incommensurable scale compared to that of the Old. Add to that the upheaval, which still affects me, of a face-to-face encounter with a virgin and immense nature, while all that I had known before was a nature of modest proportions, whose wildest aspects still betrayed the patient work of man, extending back for centuries, even millennia.

Finally—and this is perhaps the major reason—the study of no other continent, it seems to me, demands more of the imagination. America was essentially populated by people from Asia who crossed the land bridge that existed at the site of today's Bering Strait. But when? The best estimates vary by a margin of 50,000 years. And there remains not a trace of these passages, which were repeated at various times. Because of the variations in sea level, the routes are lost, either high in the coastal mountains or beneath the sea. That is not all. America offers the stupefying spectacle of very high cultures next to those of very low technical and economic levels. Furthermore, these high cultures knew only an ephemeral existence: each one was born, developed, and perished during the period of a few centuries. And the cultures that had disappeared before the arrival of the Spaniards were probably more learned and refined than the ones in their decline that the Spaniards saw—and that still astonished them.

In truth, and despite all the work that has been done, we still don't know, we still don't understand, what America was. As it was for the fifteenth- and sixteenth-century discoverers, it remains another planet. Practically each year brings a discovery that challenges everything we think we know. The state of Americanism is somewhat like that of the nineteenth-century sciences, rich in hope of discoveries within reach. That is what makes it so appealing.

D.E. But then, why, after your double failure at the Collège de France, didn't Talcott Parsons' invitation lead you to go back?

C.L.-S. It is one thing to have a passion for the New World before 1492 and another to uproot yourself to live in the New World of to-day. The Harvard invitation must have been leading me to make a choice, since before I turned it down, I went to Gaston Berger, then director of higher education, for advice. He told me, "Don't hesitate, take it." I was content with my bohemian life, I preferred going to the flea market every Saturday to living in Cambridge, Massachusetts.

On the subject of the flea market, I'll end with a story. One day Pierre Mendès-France, whom I had met in the United States, asked me to take him there. He cherished the hope of finding old documents about his family, from the time they had settled in the West Indies. Needless to say, we returned empty-handed . . .

5

The Mysteries of the Number 8

D.E. In 1955 you published *Tristes Tropiques*. What led you to write such a book?

C.L.-S. It all began with a request on the part of Jean Malaurie, whom I didn't know and who was founder of the series Terre humaine. It had never dawned on me to write about my travels.

However, in the period I was going through, I was convinced that I had no future in the university system, so the idea of just writing what came to me was tempting.

Also, as time went on, I had gained a certain distance. It was no longer a matter of transcribing a journal of my expedition. I had to rethink my old adventures, reflect upon them, and draw some kind of conclusions.

D.E. I believe you wrote *Tristes Tropiques* rather quickly.

C.L.-S. In four months. I was feeling guilty about not working on my second volume on the complex structures of kinship, which I still thought I could write. It seemed that I was interrupting my work by an intermission that had to be as short as possible. I believed I was committing a sin against science. The book bears witness to the fact, at least in the first edition, which was full of gross errors. I didn't even take the trouble to check the spelling of Portuguese words—I wrote them down the way they sounded to me. The first edition is a monstrosity.

D.E. A monstrosity that received a rather warm welcome. There were articles by Leiris, Blanchot . . .

C.L.-S. By Georges Bataille and Raymond Aron as well. Yes, it was well received, but it sold poorly. Did you know that the Académie Goncourt—the book came out just before prizes were awarded that year—published a notice stating they regretted being unable to give the award to *Tristes Tropiques* because it wasn't a novel?

I received some letters, one of which was particularly moving. It was from Pierre MacOrlan, a writer I adored during my adolescence. I knew I had written *Tristes Tropiques* with him in mind. He probably liked my book because without realizing it he found things in there that came from him.

D.E. It was a very warm reception in literary circles, then, but in anthropological circles?

C.L.-S. The reaction was more reserved. The moment he opened *Tristes Tropiques,* Paul Rivet shut the door in my face. He was quick to anger and, reading the first sentence, "Travel and travelers are two things I loathe," he must have stopped there and concluded I was a traitor. I did not see him until his last days. He was in the hospital and called me to his bedside to make peace.

D.E. But this book was nevertheless the work of an anthropologist?

C.L.-S. Whole pages were taken as is from *Family and Social Life of the Nambikwara.*

D.E. In your eyes was it a kind of synthesis of what you had done.

C.L.-S. Of what I had done up to that point, yes. Also, of everything I believed and dreamed about.

*

D.E. What was the intellectual atmosphere like in France between your return in 1948 and the publication of *Tristes Tropiques?* It was the heyday of existentialism . . .

C.L.-S. Yes, but I was far away from all that. I was reading the books but hardly knew any of the authors. I met Sartre only two or three times, and, except for a luncheon at Jean Pouillon's, by accident.

D.E. But you knew Merleau-Ponty.

C.L.-S. His election to the Collège de France closely followed my own rejection. This coincidence brought us closer. As you know, an election to the Collège occurs in several stages: the professors vote to create a chair, then a little later select the person who will hold that chair, and as a formality choose another candidate as a second possibility. The appropriate academy of the Institut de France must then give its opinion. As a rule, it purely and simply confirms the order selected by the Collège. Then everything goes to the ministry to be decided. In Merleau-Ponty's case, the Académie des Sciences

morales reversed the order of the Collège's decision and put Gaston
Berger in first place. Merleau-Ponty was unaware of these subtleties.
They had been explained to me when I was a candidate, so I was able
to help him adopt a plan of action. In fact, these ups and downs were
a help to him, for the minister, according to tradition in case of a conflict between the Collège and the Institut, hastened to decree in favor
of the first, which speeded up the normally slow process.

D.E. You became close friends.

C.L.-S. Yes, and we saw each other a lot with our wives. And also
the Lacans and the Leiris.

D.E. Did you discuss your work?

C.L.-S. We spoke little of philosophy, but Merleau-Ponty was the
one who had the idea that I should try again for the Collège. That was
as early as 1954.

I remember it clearly, because I answered: "I'm writing a book
[*Tristes Tropiques*], and when you and the professors at the Collège
read it, you won't be trying to get me elected there any longer." I had
unleashed my pen, as Métraux liked to say.

D.E. In spite of everything, he presented your candidacy in 1959.

C.L.-S. Not only did he present it, but he devoted three months of
his life to it, and he was not to live much longer. He knew very well
that there were obstacles. Faral's old group still had partisans. Merleau-
Ponty took a great deal of trouble. He called on people, wrote letters,
and did it so well that there was no other proposal for a chair in opposition to his.

D.E. The election went off without any problem?

C.L.-S. There were opposing votes, which was assured because I was
the only candidate. The electors always like to have freedom to choose.

D.E. Did your entry into the Collège change your working conditions a great deal?

C.L.-S. Of course. I forgot to say that during the period between
1953 and this election, I was holding a second position. I was secretary general of the International Council of Social Sciences, a non-
governmental organization under the aegis of UNESCO. Obviously,
that took a lot of time.

D.E. What did you do?

C.L.-S. I tried to give the impression that an organization without
goal or function had a reason for existing.

D.E. Without goal or function, but with a little money?

C.L.-S. Yes, some means, which had to be justified with a sem-blance of activity.

D.E. You received professors, researchers . . .

C.L.-S. I entertained many people. Above all, I had to organize in-ternational meetings and come up with topics of discussion.

D.E. It was in this context that you wrote *Race and History*[1] in 1952?

C.L.-S. *Race and History* is a work that UNESCO commissioned from me before I entered the Social Sciences Council. I must have written it in 1951 because it was published in 1952, before I assumed my functions at the Council. The request came via Métraux, who was at UNESCO at the time.

D.E. How did your inaugural lecture go at the Collège de France? You gave it on January 5, 1960.

C.L.-S. After such an awkward past, it went better than I could have hoped. I included passages in the lecture that could be deci-phered only by the initiated, such as the strange speculations con-cerning the number 8 that I gave at the beginning. Merleau-Ponty did not like to be reminded that we were born in the same year, 1908. He thought I seemed older, which was true. He saw himself aging in me. Moreover, and despite the generosity he displayed on my behalf, he had a hard time combating the fear that he had laid a goose egg. He thought me capable of the most outrageous inventions.

When I was rhapsodizing on all the possible relations between my chair and the number 8, I was leading him to expect—and fear—that I was coming to our shared birthdate, since the chair existed because of him. It was an innocent joke.

And then, near the end, I deplored the fact that the chair was cre-ated so late (on the pretext that it could have been given to one of the first voyagers to Brazil in the sixteenth century). This was a way of re-minding some of my new colleagues that this lecture, which they were now applauding, could have been given ten years earlier.

D.E. Was it truly the first chair in anthropology at the Collège de France?

1. Claude Lévi-Strauss, *Race et histoire* (Paris: UNESCO, 1952; reprinted Paris: Folio-essais, 1987); published in English as chap. 18 of *Structural Anthropology,* vol. 2 (New York: Basic Books, 1976).

C.L.-S. You can't exactly say the first, because there was Marcel Mauss. His chair was called sociology, but in fact it was anthropology.

D.E. What was the reaction to your lecture?

C.L.-S. Merleau-Ponty was watching the reaction of those who had been the most hostile. He told me afterward that we had won the day.

D.E. At the Collège, you met Braudel again.

C.L.-S. Whom I hadn't seen since Brazil.

D.E. And Benveniste . . .

C.L.-S. Who had been on the jury for my thesis. And Dumézil, who had gotten me into the Ecole des hautes études.

The first gathering of professors attended by the newly elected member is always a problem. They introduce you, everyone rises, you are welcomed and invited to sit down, and then you look all around you for an empty chair at this table with fifty places. Merleau-Ponty had warned me and given me a floor plan, so that I was able to go without hesitating to the place where he sat and where he had taken care to save me a chair. So I found myself between him and Benveniste.

D.E. Did you and Braudel become closer than you had been in Brazil?

C.L.-S. He was very caught up in his work and his various responsibilities. Outside of the meetings of the Collège, I can't say that we saw each other much. Except when he took on the presidency of the Sixth Section of the Ecole des hautes etudes, of which I was also a part.

D.E. Did you get along well?

C.L.-S. Deep down, Braudel was good, sensitive, and generous. You could always count on him for the big things. At the same time, he liked to dominate and couldn't resist the pleasure of gently teasing anyone who came to see him. Sometimes his tone was unsettling. He also knew how to be charming when he wanted to. Then he was a spellbinder.

D.E. Could you clarify one thing? Braudel was president of the Sixth Section of the Ecole des hautes études, while you were in the Fifth. How were you able to meet?

C.L.-S. I belonged to both sections. Indeed, I was involved in the Sixth before I entered the other. I had an indeterminate status I can no longer explain. At any rate, Lucien Febvre had asked me to give seminars at the Sixth, beginning in 1949, I believe.

D.E. When you were elected to the Fifth Section, you stayed at the Sixth?

C.L.-S. Yes, for at the time the administrative rules were very loose. The president of the Sixth virtually did what he wished. It was an enlightened monarchy.

D.E. And you continued in the two sections after you were elected to the Collège de France?

C.L.-S. I continued for several years with the Fifth Section, for somewhat longer with the Sixth. It became the Ecole des Hautes Etudes en Sciences Sociales, where I remained until I retired, but I no longer taught in it. I stayed on as director of the laboratory of social anthropology, which is associated with the CNRS, the Collège de France, and the Ecole des hautes études.

D.E. Indeed, when you entered the Collège, you founded this laboratory, which later was to grow.

C.L.-S. In the beginning we were housed in one of the outbuildings of the Musée Guimet, on Avenue d'Iéna. It was the old private mansion of Emile Guimet. With three or four coworkers I occupied a room that had once been the bathroom. Pieces of pipe still stuck out of the walls, which were covered with ceramic tile, and I had what was left of the bathtub drain under my feet. We barely had room to move. I met with visitors on the landing, where we were able to offer them two worn-out lawn chairs.

D.E. Why did they put you there?

C.L.-S. The museum had given the Fifth Section the building for the establishment of a center for religious studies, which still exists, and the section was willing to lodge my newborn laboratory in two rooms. The larger one was completely filled with the Human Relations Area Files, an enormous documentary tool issued in twenty-five copies by Yale University on behalf of the United States government. UNESCO had acquired a copy for France, on the condition that it be available to all European scholars. After many tribulations, it was entrusted to us.

D.E. At that time you took on a second role: directing a team, a laboratory.

C.L.-S. I always had done administrative work along with my scientific or intellectual undertakings. During my student years, you will recall, I was the secretary for political organizations and then for a member of the Chambre des Députés. Later I was secretary general at the Ecole libre des hautes études in New York and then cultural counsellor of the embassy. Then I held an administrative position at the Musée de l'Homme. At the International Council of Social Sciences as well.

D.E. Did you want to create the laboratory because you believed anthropological work exceeded the capacities of a single individual?

C.L.-S. No, I have always planned and done my own work alone. But I had access to a building and the resources to offer young scholars opportunities for work. Directing the laboratory was a load I carried most willingly, although I did have some secretarial help, funds for purchasing books, and the use of a photocopying machine.

D.E. Who were your colleagues at the laboratory?

C.L.-S. At the outset were Isac Chiva and Jean Pouillon. In their footsteps came Lucien Sebag, Pierre Clastres, Robert Jaulin, Françoise and Michel Izard. . . . Some of them had been working with me since I had come over from the Musée de l'Homme. For example, Lucien Bernot, who became a professor of the Collège.

Lucien Febvre had given me the task of directing, with the backing of UNESCO, research for a monograph on a French village, the first such work, I believe, to be conceived in an ethnological manner. I chose Lucien Bernot to lead it. His work there resulted in a book, *Nouville, un village français,* which appeared in the series Travaux et mémoires de l'Institut d'Ethnologie. Chiva led a research project in Corsica under the same auspices. This was the beginning of a long collaboration between the two of us, which lasted until I retired. Both the laboratory and I owe him a debt.

D.E. Shortly after the foundation of the laboratory, you had the idea for a journal, *L'Homme.*

C.L.-S. I was dismayed that France had no equivalent to the *American Anthropologist* in the United States or *Man* in Great Britain. So I wanted to ensure that *L'Homme* (a title contested at first by a men's fashion magazine that claimed ownership; we had to consult a lawyer) became a voice for all of French anthropology, not just one group. Right away we sought out colleagues with no ties to the laboratory to take part in the editorial committee.

D.E. Most notably, you asked Benveniste and Pierre Gourou.

C.L.-S. I thought it was essential for us to display characteristics that originated with French scholarship, particularly the link between ethnology and human geography as found in the tradition of Vidal de la Blache. *Les Paysans du delta tonkinois,* which made Pierre Gourou famous, is the work of an anthropologist as well as that of a geographer or historian. By inviting Benveniste, we paid homage to linguistics, particularly structural linguistics, which he represented in France and from which, in my mind, structural anthropology can never been separated. Moreover, Benveniste had reflected a great deal on the problems of kinship in the Indo-European region, and I felt close to him, even if I didn't interpret the data in the same way. But with Benveniste and Gourou, we were a bit too much of a "Collège de France" club. If *L'Homme* was to represent French anthropology, we would have to go further. So we called on André Leroi-Gourhan, Georges-Henri Rivière, and André-Georges Haudricourt.

D.E. Leroi-Gourhan was not yet at the Collège de France.

C.L.-S. He entered in 1969, to succeed Dumézil, who was retiring.

D.E. Why didn't you include any historians?

C.L.-S. There, matters were more delicate. In 1960 history and anthropology, which had become so closely associated, were, if I may say so, competing for the public's attention. I'm not sure that the historians would have been very enthusiastic about aligning themselves with a journal that did not carry their banner. Since then, things have changed, and one frequently hears of historical anthropology.

D.E. On the subject of André Haudricourt, perhaps you have read his little book of recollections that appeared not long ago. He speaks of Leroi-Gourhan and yourself and describes the "kindness" of you both. He adds, "As for Lévi-Strauss, his philosophical background made him less accessible to me. He bore no grudge for the criticisms Georges Granai and I made concerning the connections between linguistic and other structures. . . ."[2]

C.L.-S. I responded to his criticisms in *Structural Anthropology,* but I have always held Haudricourt in high regard. He has a subtle and original mind able to link the history of technology and of botany with his work in linguistics. He has offered some very penetrating insights.

---

2. André-Georges Haudricourt and Pascal Dibie, *Les Pieds sur terre* (Paris: Métailié, 1987).

D.E. André Leroi-Gourhan also speaks of his relationship with you in a book of interviews. He says, "Lévi-Strauss and I are practically opposites, but opposites that are ultimately connected. Twenty years ago we had the feeling we were different and belonged to two incompatible worlds. That went on for years. Bit by bit I understood what he was after, and he likewise. And now we support one another in friendship after enduring each other's company in suspicion. I spend my time immersed in a past that perhaps could have been replaced by the study of modern primitives, had any still existed. This doesn't keep me from taking in time the same route Claude Lévi-Strauss has taken in space. But perhaps in my case, it is not a matter of refuge, since it has been this way for me since I was twelve."[3] Do you agree with his remarks?

C.L.-S. Overall, yes. A few months ago, his students organized a colloquium in honor of his memory and asked me to say a few words. I emphasized the paradox that for many years Leroi-Gourhan and I coasted along rather than really becoming acquainted, while there were a number of common points between our ways of seeing and thinking. I compared some of our texts, and it was striking. For each of us, our work always consisted in finding invariants.

D.E. So you have the feeling that he did in time what you did in space?

C.L.-S. He also did it in space for times past. And even from your perspective, the analogies with my work are clear. The idea he developed throughout his work—that the evolution of tools, of utensils, generally speaking of everything related to techniques, has an impersonal quality, arising independently among the various forms of humanity—closely resembles what I said about myth. Unfortunately, in French anthropology there reigns an atmosphere we have inherited from our forebears, a climate of mutual suspicion. Each one jealously stakes out what he considers to be his own domain. For a long time, Leroi-Gourhan didn't trust me.

D.E. He was a prehistorian, but a large part of his work deals with anthropology.

3. André Leroi-Gourhan, *Les Racines du monde*. Interviews with Claude-Henri Rocquet (Paris: Belfond, 1982), p. 109.

C.L.-S. He always maintained that the two could not be separated. But if a freer climate had prevailed among Leroi-Gourhan, Louis Dumont, myself, and some others, who were doing related things in different disciplines, French anthropology would have gained a great deal in strength and influence—even though, on that account, we don't have too much to complain about. Let's hope our successors have learned the lesson.

D.E. What do you think of his statement implying that anthropology was a refuge for you?

C.L.-S. For many anthropologists, perhaps, not just myself, the ethnological vocation is a flight from civilization, from a century in which one doesn't feel at home. That is not the case for everyone. Margaret Mead, for example, felt a part of her society and her time. She wanted to serve her contemporaries. If I have occasionally made similar statements, I was not speaking from the heart.

D.E. For you, anthropology is not a way to serve?

C.L.-S. I am not saying that it cannot serve. But it isn't what I ask of it, it's not the part of it that satisfies me.

D.E. Are you still actively involved in the journal you founded in 1961, *L'Homme?*

C.L.-S. Not any more. Don't forget that one or two generations have come along since my own. If *L'Homme* is to continue to speak for French anthropology, younger people must take on the responsibility. So I have withdrawn. But from time to time I still publish articles and reviews there. Jean Pouillon keeps the tradition alive with his talent and devotion.

6

Structuralism in Paris

D.E. In 1958, a year before your election to the Collège de France, you published *Structural Anthropology,*[1] a collection of articles written since 1945.

C.L.-S. I had been thinking about it for some time, and before writing *Tristes Tropiques* I took the book, or rather the idea for the book, to Gallimard. I talked to Brice Parain, who turned me down. He told me my ideas hadn't matured. After *Tristes Tropiques,* Gaston Gallimard turned on the charm to get me back. Plon had already welcomed me; I've stayed with them.

D.E. Did you know that a few years later Brice Parain refused Michel Foucault's *Madness and Civilization?*

C.L.-S. I didn't know that. That's a consolation.

D.E. The title of the book, *Structural Anthropology,* was a veritable red flag. Was it meant as a manifesto?

C.L.-S. The title seemed obvious. I had found I was doing structuralism as the linguists did. But don't forget that structuralism was not yet what fashion was to make of it. I simply meant that I placed myself in the same intellectual province as Saussure, Troubetzkoy, Jakobson, Benveniste—at least, that was my ambition.

D.E. In any event, it's a title that brought you fortune.

C.L.-S. Bad as well as good!

D.E. Are you sorry you gave it that title?

C.L.-S. Not at all. But the vogue for structuralism unleashed all manner of unfortunate results. The term was besmirched; illegitimate, sometimes ridiculous applications were made of it. There was nothing I could do.

1. Claude Lévi-Strauss, *Anthropologie structurale* (Paris: Plon, 1958); English edition, *Structural Anthropology* (New York: Basic Books, 1963).

D.E. How did you choose the articles for the collection? You left out quite a few, notably "Le Père Noël supplicié," which appeared in *Les Temps modernes* in 1951.

C.L.-S. I included articles of a similar level of difficulty, which seemed to reflect a common ground. I thought the one you mentioned was on the light side, a bit journalistic. It would have disrupted the tone of the work. For all that, I don't repudiate it.

D.E. You often say that you don't like getting involved in debates, but there is a piece in *Strutural Anthropology* that is polemical from beginning to end.[2]

C.L.-S. I was younger and more inclined to react. I was smarting under attacks and criticisms. With age, this fervor weakens. On the other hand, so many books and articles have been devoted to me—often unfriendly ones—that were I to succumb to debates, they would take up all my time. I'd do nothing else.

D.E. Do you read the criticisms leveled against you?

C.L.-S. By accident, for the people who attack my work—particularly the English and the Americans—generally avoid sending me their books. I learn of their existence through professional journals that mention them or review them two or three years later. To read and discuss them then would seem old hat.

D.E. What are your feelings when you read something about yourself?

C.L.-S. When it is hostile, I'm irritated, because I tell myself that I ought to clear up the factual errors, dispel the misunderstandings. However, I resent the author of such remarks less than the temptation he inspires in me to drop my work to respond. And then, after being stirred up for a moment, I calm down, knowing that I wouldn't change his mind. Still, sometimes, in the presence of obvious errors or bad faith, I find I must put a stop to it. But does it do any good? I believe so less and less.

D.E. Was the piece against Gurvitch, Rodinson, and Revel in *Structural Anthropology* especially written for the publication of the volume?

C.L.-S. I knew Gurvitch at the Ecole libre des hautes études of New York, where he also taught. At the beginning we got on very well

2. *Structural Anthropology,* chap. 16.

together. He once asked me to write a chapter on French sociology for a compendium to be called *La Sociologie au xx* ^e *siècle.* [3]

D.E. And did you mention him there?

C.L.-S. Of course. I went to a great deal of trouble to understand him, and he said that there had never been anything better written about him.

D.E. He dominated the sociology of the day?

C.L.-S. Less than he thought.

D.E. But he was very powerful.

C.L.-S. He became a professor at the Sorbonne. And then, he had an anxious temperament and was prone to extreme touchiness, which occasionally led to violent reactions that people feared. He could nurse a grudge forever. Particularly since he was firmly persuaded that he had brought about a complete renewal of sociological thought. Gurvitch's contribution was hardly negligeable, but his imagination magnified it.

D.E. And he wrote an article against you to which you responded in chapter 16 of *Structural Anthropology.* [4]

C.L.-S. His attack was a total surprise. Everything led me to believe that our relationship was based on understanding, even friendship. I ought to have paid more attention to a signal; after asking me to write an introduction to the selected works of Marcel Mauss in a collection he was editing, he was careful to keep his distance. He obviously didn't like my introduction. After reading it, he added a short postscript to the proofs in which his feelings were clear. That was when things between us began to go bad. [5]

D.E. How did he react to your reply of 1958?

C.L.-S. We didn't see each other again.

D.E. In the same article, you respond to a book by Jean-François Revel, *Pourquoi des philosophes?* [6] The fact that he had devoted almost an entire chapter of a book to you in 1957 shows that your name had begun to reach more than just a narrow circle of specialists.

3. *La Sociologie au xxe siècle,* ed. G. Gurvitch and W. E. Moore (Paris: Presses Universitaires de France, 1947).

4. Georges Gurvitch, "Le concept de structure sociale," *Cahiers internationaux de sociologie* 19, no. 2 (1955).

5. Marcel Mauss, *Sociologie et anthropologie,* introduction by Claude Lévi-Strauss and preface by Georges Gurvitch (Paris: Presses Universitaires de France, 1950).

6. Jean-Francois Revel, *Pourquoi des philosophes?* (Paris: Julliard, 1957).

C.L.-S. That happened after *Structural Anthropology*. Not that this book reached the public, but it was noticed and commented on by philosophers, sociologists, historians. . . .

*

D.E. *Totemism*[7] and *The Savage Mind*,[8] the two books that followed in 1962, signaled a new departure in your research.

C.L.-S. I believe I would have to put that departure somewhat earlier, when I was elected to the Fifth Section of the Ecole des hautes études. This section is devoted to religious studies. Now, up until that time I had been chiefly concerned with marriage rules and kinship systems. Overnight, I changed my objective. So you are right in a way. These books of 1962 are important for me because I began a second stage, by far the longest, of my career, devoted to the study of religious representations. In a way it was a prelude to the Mythology series.

D.E. In both cases these works take a negative approach, stripping away old material, if I may put it that way.

C.L.-S. I wouldn't say negative. Rather they are critiques in the Kantian sense. I needed to free anthropology from certain illusions that obscured the study of religion in preliterate societies. I needed to grapple with defining the problem that would occupy me during the coming years.

D.E. The fashion for "structuralism" began with *The Savage Mind*.

C.L.-S. For me that's secondary. Moreover, I never measured its extent. If I had set about exploiting that fashion, I might have won a larger place in contemporary thought, but the cost wasn't worth it to me.

D.E. But you played the game! You gave quite a few interviews. You didn't refuse the chances you were given to speak up.

C.L.-S. Perhaps that is true for the early years. I soon withdrew into my shell.

D.E. In the 1960s and 1970s, people spoke of "structuralism" as if it were a worldwide phenomenon, and the same list of names always occurred: Lévi-Strauss, Foucault, Lacan, Barthes. . . .

7. See chap. 1 n. 2 above.
8. Claude Lévi-Strauss, *La Pensée sauvage* (Paris: Plon, 1962); English edition, *The Savage Mind* (Chicago: University of Chicago Press, 1966).

C.L.-S. That still bothers me, as there are no grounds for that combination. I don't see what these names have in common. Or rather I do see it: it is deceptive. I feel I belong to another intellectual family, the one represented by Benveniste, Dumézil. I feel as close to Jean-Pierre Vernant and the people who work with him. Foucault was comppletely right in rejecting the comparison.

D.E. What was your relationship with him like?

C.L.-S. We saw one another from afar at the assemblies at the Collège, and once François Jacob had us together for dinner. That is all. Of course, I read his books, which he had the kindness to send me.

His work touches me because of its stylistic qualities—I recall his inaugural lecture at the Collège de France. It was very beautiful in a literary way, tinged with feeling. On the other hand, I have reservations about an attitude that seems to repeat at every turn, Watch out, things are not as you believe, it is the other way around. In a word, an attitude that says that black is white and white is black. This enlightens me concerning the author's opinions, but tells me nothing else: a photographic negative and positive both contain the same amount of information.

I also have a hard time resisting the impression—I won't try to justify it—that Foucault takes some liberties with chronology. As if he knew beforehand what he wanted to prove and then sought to support his thesis. In a historian of ideas, that bothers me. Perhaps I'm wrong. It's a point on which only professional historians can pronounce.

Even so, he played a positive role by giving back an entire generation confidence in philosophy. He convinced his disciples that a philosophy ailing from existentialism could make a fresh start on the condition that it be methodically applied to the study of concrete objects.

D.E. You, too, found this to be your route?

C.L.-S. Of course not. I never aspired to develop a foundation for philosophical thought. It is true that, in my own past, what drew me away from philosophy toward anthropology was precisely the awareness that if you wish to understand man you must avoid becoming mired in introspection or limiting yourself to studying only one society—our own—or again to surveying a few centuries of the Western world. I wanted to base this understanding on the most different and distant cultural experiences. Foucault's work was completely different, for he was exclusively interested in our culture, including its past.

D.E. And how about Barthes? What was your relationship with him? A few years ago they republished a small article you addressed to him on the subject of *S/Z*.

C.L.-S. I wrote it as a joke. I didn't like *S/Z*. His comments seemed to me far too much like those of Professor Libellule[9] in Muller and Reboux's *Just Like Racine*. So, a bit sarcastically and to avoid any awkwardness I sent him these few pages in which I "overdid it," in place of the compliments I felt incapable of making. He took it seriously. I was asked to publish it. Why not? I said yes.[10]

D.E. Have you read his other books?

C.L.-S. Of course. But I never felt close to him, and this feeling was confirmed by his later development. Late in life Barthes went completely against what he had done before, which, I'm convinced, was far from his true nature.

D.E. You knew Lacan very well.

C.L.-S. We were very close for a number of years. We used to go with the Merleau-Pontys for lunch at Guitrancourt, where Lacan had a country house. Once, my wife and I wanted to find a hideaway in the country, and Lacan had just bought a new car he wanted to take on the road. The four of us took off together. It was a lot of fun. You should have seen Lacan descending upon a shabby provincial hotel, in his most regal manner ordering that his bath be run that very instant!

We hardly ever talked about psychoanalysis or philosophy; instead it was usually art and literature. His knowledge was vast. He used to buy paintings and works of art, and this was a subject of our conversations.

D.E. When you begin your courses in the Fifth Section of the Ecole des hautes études, he was beginning his famous "seminar." Did you ever have occasion to attend?

C.L.-S. Later on and only once, the first one that he held on Rue d'Ulm. When he was shut out of the Ecole Normale, even though I was convinced he was to blame, I intervened with Braudel for the Ecole des Hautes études to give him a place.

D.E. What do you think of his work?

C.L.-S. I would have to understand it. And I always had the impression that to his fervent admirers, "understand" means some-

---

9. "Libellule" = "dragonfly."—Trans.
10. At the end of a volume entitled *Claude Lévi-Strauss* (Paris: Gallimard, 1979).

thing other than it does to me. It would have taken me five or six lectures. Merleau-Ponty and I used to talk about it and concluded that we didn't have the time.

D.E. Still, you quoted him . . .

C.L.-S. Only once, I think, and that was primarily out of friendship.

D.E. Despite your friendship you were annoyed that his name was linked with yours in the "structuralist" pantheon.

C.L.-S. I admit it. But by then he had become a kind of guru, and our ties had weakened a great deal.

D.E. In *L'Histoire de la psychanalyse*[11] Elisabeth Roudinesco states that Lacan was always very unhappy about his lack of a university position, particularly that he wasn't at the Collège de France.

C.L.-S. He never mentioned it, but it is possible.

D.E. You never had the idea of presenting him as a candidate at the Collège de France?

C.L.-S. It never crossed my mind. And, as I just said, he never breathed a word of it to me or ever said anything about it to Merleau-Ponty in my presence.

11. Elisabeth Roudinesco, *La Bataille de cent ans,* vol. 2 (Paris: Seuil, 1986); English edition, *Jacques Lacan and Co.,* trans. Jeffrey Mehlman (Chicago: University of Chicago Press, 1990).

7

The Collège de France

D.E. The Collège de France is a place of prestige, the pinnacle of a university career. Yet you told me the other day that your entire career had been outside the traditional university environment.

C.L.-S. It is a prestigious place, but truly, from the time of its creation by Francis I, it has remained and was always intended to remain outside the university. Earlier I had taught in Brazil, in the United States, then in France at the Ecole des hautes études. But never in the university.

D.E. What were the advantages of working outside of the traditional university system?

C.L.-S. More freedom and, in a sense, tolerance for a less regimented spirit. Having to follow a curriculum, give examinations, serve on thesis committees (which occasionally I cannot avoid)—these specific and regular obligations bore me. At the Collège a professor's sole obligation is to present a new subject every year. That was perfect for me.

D.E. It was a freedom that paid off for you, since, as you recall in the preface to *Paroles données*,[1] your courses often became books.

C.L.-S. From the time I entered the Collège my teaching and my books grew apace. I mean, there were always some modifications, but the courses at the Collège were my testing ground.

D.E. You taught there from 1960 to 1982. What events marked that long period?

C.L.-S. The most important was undoubtedly the installation of the anthropology laboratory in the buildings of the Collège.

1. *Paroles donñees*, pp. 11–12.

I remember that during my visits as a candidate in 1959, I had gone to see the gentleman who held the chair in geology. His laboratory was on the top floor, in a wing of the building constructed at the end of the eighteenth century by Chalgrin. In addition to the professor's office and some attics, basically there were two large and majestic rooms where a few isolated individuals could be found working at big oak tables. Along the walls, the corners of which were graced with pilasters, were mahogany cabinets, high enough to lean on, rather plain but admirably designed and proportioned. Under the Restoration these must have represented the *ne plus ultra* of what today we call office furniture. I learned that they contained the mineral collections of Louis XVIII.

Apparently the holder of the chair was a monarchist. For that reason, perhaps, he was pleased that his laboratory kept a whiff of the air of the old days. A lifesize black marble bust of Henry IV stared at him from across the huge office. The windows looked out onto century-old trees.

I was seized with a sudden desire. Nowhere else, I thought, would I rather spend my days than in these spacious, silent, and secret rooms, which still retained the aura of a mid-nineteenth-century library or laboratory. That was how I saw the Collège de France I aspired to enter: the workplace of Claude Bernard, Ernest Renan. . . .

Fate decreed that shortly afterward the chair in Mediterranean geology became vacant. The assembly of professors decided to replace it with a chair in astronomy. Even on the top floor under the rooftops, the geology laboratory was not close enough to the sky to offer the new member the kind of space he needed! Marcel Bataillon, at the time administrator of the Collège, had the idea of putting us there, and the assembly of professors agreed. So the miracle I had never dared hope for when I first entered that place of my dreams came to pass.

When we left Emile Guimet's old mansion on the Avenue d'Iéna, where we were temporarily housed, for our new location, the precious mahogany furniture and the mineral collections were taken to Meudon, to an estate bequeathed to the Collège by Marcelin Berthelot. Our library went into one of the two large rooms, the "Centre documentaire d'ethnologie comparée" (the name we gave to the thousands of Human Relations Area Files that had come from Yale) into the other. Unfortunately it was necessary to add some partitions, especially under the Mansard roof, to create individual cubicles. The noise of the typewriters and people talking would have made working together in one room impossible. But I wanted at least to keep the professor's office intact, with its old-fashioned enclosed bookcases and woodwork painted to look like oak. That was a job for a real craftsman, which added to the cost. Redoing the whole area was hardly a luxury; it hadn't been repainted in eighty years.

D.E. The anthropology laboratory remained in the "old" Collège during the whole time you taught there.

C.L.-S. Yes. But we quickly ran into difficulties. There were both personnel and scientific problems, as we had expanded to include more than thirty people. Since we lacked office space, half the scholars had to work at home or wait until one of their more fortunate colleagues left for the field so he or she could have a table for a few months. The library was growing; we had no place for new books. Above all, as subscribers to the HRAF, we continued to receive pounds and pounds of cards from Yale. To file them into the cabinets stacked on top of one another until they reached over our heads would have threatened the old flooring with their weight. Unopened packages piled up in all the corners. Now, the card index to the Files, which some people have unwisely denigrated, is above all a library: thousands of books and articles are indexed there, page by page, and even line by line, photocopied *in extenso*. Access to this bibliographic treasure, which we were supposed to keep open to all, was becoming more and more limited.

Then another miracle took place. In 1977, the president of the Republic gave the Collège a part of the old buildings of the Ecole Polytechnique, which are located on the Montagne Sainte-Geneviève. The Collège decided to put several of its laboratories for the human sciences, ours included, together in this space. In this way, we doubled our floorspace. It took seven years of labor to obtain the funds and complete the remodeling, but again I was able, before retiring in 1982, to oversee the outfitting of a place that had a distinguished history of its own and to take care that the cast-iron architecture and the decoration of the venerable Arago amphitheater—which was to become our library and around which our offices would be distributed—were respected.

Françoise Héritier-Augé, who holds the chair of comparative African studies and was called to succeed me as the director of the laboratory, moved into the new quarters in the spring of 1985, surrounded by an even larger team. She offered to have me remain as a member. The laboratory of social anthropology, founded in 1960, began its third life.

D.E. You didn't continue your responsibilities at the laboratory after you retired from teaching?

C.L.-S. No! On the contrary, I am very careful to be no more than a co-worker and, now that I am retired, even more discreet than my still active comrades. When I was young I knew too many older people who refused to let go, and I promised myself it would never happen to me. But I don't refuse to speak up if I am asked.

D.E. How did your laboratory—for at the time it truly was "your" laboratory—fare during the upheavals of May 1968?

C.L.-S. The Collège de France was shaken, although nothing very serious took place there. It was a special case. By its constitution, the Collège de France is more like an academy than a university; it consists of fifty professors who administer themselves. There was apparently even a special costume, though I have never seen it worn, that emphasized the difference: instead of the university gown, it resembled what the members of the Institut wear except that the embroidery was violet.

However, working conditions changed, especially for those in scientific disciplines who, needing collaborators, have found them for the most part at the CNRS and other organizations outside the Collège. The scientists built laboratories and work in larger and larger teams. During the sixties, in addition to the professors, the Collège remunerated or welcomed a thousand collaborators of different rank who wished to be recognized as part of the establishment, have a voice in chapter meetings, and take part in management. Their claims had a basis in the context of each laboratory. Formulated in opposition to the Collège, they completely changed the nature of the institution.

D.E. Did the problem also arise in your team?

C.L.-S. At the laboratory of social anthropology a leftist spirit reigned, and above all a feminist spirit, for there were more women than men. When I became aware the wheels were turning, I withdrew to my house under a variety of pretexts, and left them to themselves. There was a week of internal agitation, and then they came to look for me.

D.E. Raymond Aron in his *Mémoires* quotes a letter you wrote to him in October 1968. You were commenting on the university situation and, in passing, you speak of your laboratory and its way of working as "without distinction in rank or function."[2]

C.L.-S. That helped us a great deal in overcoming the crisis. At the outset, the laboratory was small, and it didn't seem useful to me to set up management structures. The full laboratory used to meet periodically. Everyone took part on a completely equal footing, down to and including the cleaning woman. We formed a direct democracy. What rights were there to assert? The system functioned to everyone's general satisfaction until my departure. It would still function that way if the CNRS hadn't imposed its more complicated administrative rules.

D.E. Were you attacked as a scholar during the upheavals in May 1968?

C.L.-S. Not at any time.

D.E. And what of the feminist militants?

C.L.-S. One or two of the women got stirred up and were asked to leave the laboratory. By general consensus, moreover.

D.E. During this time how did things go between you and the other professors at the Collège?

C.L.-S. Positions within the Collège were complicated by a difference in attitude between those in the "hard" sciences and the rest. A biologist or a physicist needs a laboratory to work. For a "literary" laboratory director such as myself, that was not the case; if the laboratory had suddenly ceased to exist, nothing or very little in my work would have changed. So my views were the opposite of those of my scientist colleagues. They were seeking a solution acceptable both to them and to the members of their teams. I was pleading in favor of separation: on the one side, the Collège as it should be, that is, a restricted community of fifty professors; on the other, the laboratories, which would be organized however the participants wished. The Collège, properly speaking, had no reason to be involved with these laboratories, except regarding their budgetary allocations if the director

2. Raymond Aron, *Mémoires* (Paris: Julliard, 1983), p. 494.

were one of the professors, and the conditions of their housing, if it provided space for them.

D.E. More generally speaking, what was your life like in May of 1968?

C.L.-S. I walked around the occupied buildings of the Sorbonne. With an ethnographer's eye. I also took part in several discussion groups with friends. There were a couple of meetings at my home.

D.E. But you didn't take a stand regarding the events?

C.L.-S. No. Once the first moment of curiosity had worn off, once the strangeness had become tiresome, I found May 1968 repugnant.

D.E. Why?

C.L.-S. Because I can't accept cutting down trees for barricades (trees are life, and life is to be respected), turning public places that benefit everyone and are the responsibility of all into trash heaps, or scrawling graffiti on university buildings or elsewhere. Nor can I accept bringing intellectual work and the management of institutions to a halt because of a war of words.

D.E. Still it was a time when things were seething, a time of innovation and imagination. That part of it must have attracted you.

C.L.-S. I'm sorry to disappoint you, but not at all. For me, May 1968 was symptomatic of yet another step downward in the deterioration of the university, which began a long time ago. Even while at the lycée I used to say that my generation, myself included, could not bear comparison with that of Bergson, Proust, and Durkheim at the same age. I don't believe that May 1968 destroyed the university but rather that May 1968 took place because the university was destroying itself.

D.E. Doesn't your hostility toward May 1968 mark a complete break with your youthful political engagement?

C.L.-S. If I were to seek the signs of this break, I would find them much earlier, in the final pages of *Tristes Tropiques*. I remember that I was still trying my best to maintain a link with my ideological and political past. When I reread these pages, they have a false ring to them. The break was made a long time ago.

D.E. A while back I was speaking of a letter you wrote to Raymond Aron. When did you get to know him?

C.L.-S. I don't remember. It had to be after the war. Before then, I might have glimpsed him at the Brunschvicg's, who invited guests on Sunday mornings. I went there a couple of times.

D.E. The fact that you corresponded with him shows there was some common ground.

C.L.-S. Our relations were based on mutual feeling, but I cannot say that we were truly close. We wrote to one another on several occasions. I must have a few of his letters.

D.E. You know the famous saying, "It is better to be wrong with Sartre than right with Aron." Were you more on the side of those who preferred to "be right with Aron"?

C.L.-S. No doubt about that.

D.E. When Raymond Aron died, you declared that he was "an upright thinker."[3] Did you follow his work?

C.L.-S. I didn't read his articles on a regular basis, but when I came across one I was struck by the clarity of his thinking, the subtlety of his judgments.

D.E. In this same interview, you were speaking against Sartre, whose mind you described, on the contrary, as "false."

C.L.-S. Yes, of course, but Sartre had genius, a word I would not apply to Aron. Sartre was a being unto himself, with enormous talent, capable of achieving fame in a wide variety of literary genres. That said, his case proves to a striking degree that a superior intellect may talk nonsense if it wishes to predict the course of history and, still worse, play a role in it. The intellect can only do as Aron did, to try to understand after the fact. The virtues of the people who make history are of a completely different type.

3. *Le Nouvel Observateur,* October 21, 1983, pp. 96–97.

8

The Académie française

D.E. In 1973 you were elected to the Académie française. In your responding remarks to Alain Pyrefitte later on, when he too was welcomed as a member of this body,[1] you stated that the idea of belonging to the Académie "never crossed my mind." How did it come to pass?

C.L.-S. For several years off and on people had been giving me signals, which in the beginning I didn't take seriously. The first person to mention it was André Chamson. I had known him for a long time. From 1928 to 1930 he was the secretary of the radical group at the Palais-Bourbon. Déat, secretary of the socialist group, had the office next door to him, and I would often stop by. Chamson's family property was located in the Cévennes region, three or four kilometers from the house my parents owned. After the armistice in 1940, both of us were holed up in the Cévennes, so we used take walks together and discuss what was going on in the world. After the war we took up where we left off. That was when Chamson spoke to me about the Académie. It seemed unbelievable to me, so I chalked it up to pure kindness and paid no further attention.

Then an eminent personality I barely knew entered the scene: Wladimir d'Ormesson, who wrote to me once or twice. Again, I turned a deaf ear. Finally, after Montherlant died, Jean d'Ormesson organized a meeting with Maurice Druon. Ormesson was not yet a member of the Académie, but he had charmed me with his talent and had been a neighbor when I was on the International Council of Social Sciences at UNESCO, which is a sister organization to the Inter-

1. *Discours de réception d'Alain Peyrefitte et réponse de Claude Lévi-Strauss* (Paris: Gallimard, 1977), p. 57.

national Council of Philosophy and the Human Sciences, which he
still directs. Both of them told me, Now is the time, go ahead. They
insisted that I go see Maurice Genevoix, then life secretary, which is
what I did. He told me the same thing. I sent the letter announcing
my candidacy the day before I left for British Columbia.

D.E. You were the only candidate.

C.L.-S. Another one withdrew.

D.E. So it went off without a hitch.

C.L.-S. Yes, but it was hardly a triumph! I was elected on the first
vote, with a majority of exactly one.

D.E. What was the reaction of the people around you?

C.L.-S. Very negative. Not from my wife or my sons, but my colleagues and friends didn't understand. They felt I was betraying
them. They had a mythical idea of the Académie. They thought I was
going to abandon them, move into another sphere.

D.E. Also, I suppose, there was a kind of hostility toward the institution itself. . . .

C.L.-S. Yes, and I found that a little childish. Since I was fond of
them, I wanted to justify myself. So the first part of my acceptance
speech, where I compared American Indian rites to those of our own
societies, was meant for them. Aron, who was at the ceremony, told
me, "Your speech is good, but you overdid it, because everyone expected something of the sort." What he didn't see was that these
words weren't addressed to the Académie or the public but to my colleagues and collaborators. I was saying to them that, when you spend
your life studying the rites of faraway populations, there is no reason
not to view with the same care the rites of the society where you were
born and now live. Since I was speaking to anthropologists, I had to
support my arguments.

D.E. The following objection could be made: one can appreciate
institutions, watch them operate, and study them without wanting to
take part in them.

C.L.-S. Of course, but it would be hypocritical to fail to recognize
that, if these institutions call on you, it is because they are of the
opinion that you could be useful, in some modest way, to their con-
tinuation. Like it or not, you have a responsibility and can no longer
be a mere spectator.

It was Montherlant's seat. He had held and continued, after his death, to hold such an important place in the Académie that it was hard to find someone of his ilk. The Académie preferred a change. Had there ever been an anthropologist in the Académie? The originality of their choice was more striking than the person selected to fill the role. It was an ingenious solution.

Other than *Les Jeunes filles,* I had read very little of Montherlant's work. It was my duty to give his eulogy. I read all his books and took notes and developed a sincere admiration for the author of the *Célibataires* and *La Rose de sable,* and also for him as a thinker, despite what has been said about that. So nothing stood in my way, neither the figure of my predecessor nor my own presence in this three-hundred-and-fifty-year-old institution, which for its age alone inspires respect.

D.E. In fact, in the short speech you gave when Fernand Braudel received his academician's sword, you mentioned the long history of the Académie in your praises. Was this because you were in the presence of Fernand Braudel, or does this longevity truly fascinate you?

C.L.-S. We should not underestimate rites or their history. A society can only maintain itself if its members are unconditionally attached to its values. For this to occur, these values must have a sensuous aspect that protects them against reason's attempts to undermine them. At Oxford and Cambridge, and in England generally, I admire a society that still knows how to leave a place for ritual. In France the Académie is one of the last holdouts. I believed it my duty as a citizen and an anthropologist to help keep it alive.

D.E. When you were inducted into the Académie, Roger Caillois had the task of giving the traditional speech. He covered you with laurels throughout his remarks but at the end let fly a few barbed comments. It seems rather odd.

C.L.-S. It's a long story. I had heard a great deal about Caillois at the time of my travels in Brazil because Jean Marx at the Quai d'Orsay, who directed what today is called the office of cultural relations and who would later become my colleague in the Fifth Section at the Ecole des hautes études, where he taught Celtic religions, thought the world of Caillois. He spoke his name with such a flourish that at first I thought it was spelled something like Khaillouah . . .

The first time I met Caillois was in New York, when I was cultural counsellor. I invited him to give a talk at the cultural counsellor's office. I didn't like the talk, which was largely directed against my friends the surrealists and in which he called for a "return to intellectual and moral order."

I had not seen Caillois again when he published an implausible article criticizing my pamphlet *Race and History,* which I wrote, as you will recall, for UNESCO. It made me very angry, and I answered him accordingly—in those days I still believed you had to answer such things—with an article in *Les Temps modernes* called "Diogène couché." [2]

D.E. What was the basis of his argument?

C.L.-S. He spoke of the absolute superiority of Western civilization and condemned my relativism. You get the idea! My answer was scathing. Now, when I was a candidate for the Académie (where he had preceded me by two years), I learned that he supported me. This touched me. Once I was elected, I asked him to give the reception speech, saying that the only way I could thank him was to give him the last word. He feigned reluctance, then accepted.

I thought that this would put our unpleasant past to rest. Not at all. Caillois took up his old grudge and gave a speech with an ending that had the grating effect you mentioned (the first draft was even more acrimonious). Nonetheless, we remained cordial until his premature death.

Caillois was a man of great culture, curious about those unexpected connections that occur, as he used to say, "on the diagonal." He had taken Marcel Mauss's courses and been inspired by them. We ought to have gotten along. But he abandoned research in favor of style. He wanted to present his speculations in a literary or poetic mode. Form interested him more than substance. He had no tolerance for those who attempted to deal with the substance objectively and with some rigor. By a strange irony, he was reversing, but still in a conservative way, the terms of his old quarrel with the surrealists.

D.E. Do you attend the meetings of the Académie?

C.L.-S. Somewhat regularly.

D.E. What happens there?

2. "Diogène couché," in *Les Temps modernes* 195 (1955).

C.L.-S. Internal matters are debated, and then we move on to the dictionary, which is a bit like being in school again. Defining a word with precision is a very good intellectual exercise. It offers a gauge of the extent to which we make approximate or even faulty use of the language in our daily lives. I often discover technical terms I did not know. I have always hated having to hunt for clumsy and awkward paraphrases when I talk with workmen, while they have precise terms for every tool, part, and gesture of their trade. I think it is beneficial to establish such terminology and make it available; on another level, I think it is sound practice to avoid borrowing from English or American (not that I oppose this in principle) if there is a perfectly good French word, now forgotten, that says exactly the same thing. Generally, I am consulted for ethnographic terms. Believe me, defining a word such as "boomerang" in three lines without committing the same blunders that all dictionaries do requires some thought.

Language is the tool of those who write; it is complicated and difficult to handle. It is well to know its resources and limitations, and in this realm the work is unending. Compiling a dictionary is like training to an athlete or scales to a musician. The dictionary is probably just as necessary for the people who work on it as for those who consult the end product. At least, that is the way I see it.

D.E. It has been said that you were the author of the 1984 declaration of the Académie française against the proposals of the commission set up by Yvette Roudy, then minister for women's rights, to create feminine forms of certain words.

C.L.-S. I wielded the pen. The issues raised by the Roudy commission were not trivial. They concerned the future of the language.

D.E. Changing the language goes against your principles?

C.L.-S. If such changes are dictated by the whim of fashion, of course. The Académie functions legitimately when it observes usages and eventually sanctions them (a verb that I don't use in the incorrect sense given it today: to sanction means to approve, not to punish). I'm not against adopting certain feminine derivatives if they are current usage and are not contrary to the spirit of the language or the rules of word-formation. What seems unacceptable to me is to bow to a pressure group and promulgate words by decree. Especially when it is the result of something as blatant as the confusion between sex and grammatical gender. Dumézil wrote an outstanding article on the subject in the *Nouvel Observateur* that is worth handing down to posterity.[3]

D.E. In that case, one could argue that the same goes for "franglais"; since usage has imposed the use of "weekend," why should we say "fin de semaine"?

C.L.-S. I don't agree. There is a distinction. As I was saying a moment ago, we are importing English words when we have French words for the task that we have simply forgotten. We only have to put them back into circulation. French anthropologists thought they had to use the English term "sibling" to refer to the children of the same parents without reference to their sex. I showed them that that is the exact meaning of the French word *germain* ("cousins germains" are cousins so close that they can be likened to brothers or sisters). After that, only people who were behind the times still wrote "sibling."

In other cases there is no French word or else the French word has to be deformed to be applicable to something we don't have in France and have imported. In such cases let's adopt the foreign term as is or make it French. Language has always been enriched in that way. French is full of borrowed words, some of which I used to find in the mouths of the Indians of Central Brazil!

Also, we must fight against corruption of our syntax by English. I have seen too many doctoral dissertations in which the authors, force-fed on Anglo-Saxon scientific literature, know only the verb "to be" and write using only the passive voice.

D.E. Since you lived in New York, your English is fluent. Have you learned many other languages?

C.L.-S. No. I don't have a gift for languages. I write articles in faulty English, and I can give a talk in English with a hateful accent.

D.E. Doesn't this lack of facility bother you?

C.L.-S. Yes, a great deal.

D.E. You never had, like Dumézil, the relentless drive to learn languages? A consuming passion for foreign languages?

C.L.-S. For Dumézil, it was not only a passion or a drive, it was a gift! When Dumézil says he had only to take a text and a line-by-line translation, and after a hundred pages he knew the language in question, I'm awestruck.

---

3. Georges Dumézil, *Le Nouvel Observateur*, September 7, 1984, pp. 74–76.

D.E. Did you try to learn Portuguese when you were in Brazil?

C.L.-S. Of course, but at the time it wasn't absolutely necessary, because any educated Brazilian spoke French. In the field, I spoke Portuguese with the peasants of the interior. It was a rustic Portuguese, almost a patois.

D.E. And Japanese? These days you are especially interested in Japan.

C.L.-S. I tried to learn Japanese over the past ten years. But I'm too old. It goes in one ear and out the other.

D.E. Do you like to travel?

C.L.-S. I've had to travel a lot, but I don't like traveling per se. I heartily subscribe to what Madame de Staël wrote in *Corinne,* "No matter what people say, traveling is one of the saddest of life's pleasures."

D.E. So the statement, "Travel is a thing I loathe," at the opening of *Tristes Tropiques* wasn't simply a jest. . . .

C.L.-S. It was a little provocative, of course. Still it is true that, except when I was young (in those days you still could truly go "away"), traveling has never appealed to me. During the past ten years I've begun to take trips again to fill in the gaps. There are a few left . . .

D.E. Where have you gone?

C.L.-S. To Mexico, California, Israel, Italy, Korea, four trips to Japan, where I'm getting ready to go again.

D.E. What do you do when you arrive in a place like Japan?

C.L.-S. Fulfill my obligations by giving one, two, or three talks, then tour the country following an itinerary I helped to work out. I've seen a great deal of it.

D.E. What draws you there?

C.L.-S. An extremely old civilization that has a surprising symmetry with our own, but inverted. Don't forget that Japan lies on the eastern edge of the Eurasian continent just as France lies on the western edge. The two countries seem to turn their backs on one another, on each end of an immense territory that has been inhabited for thousands of years and where men and ideas have circulated unendingly. In Japan I have the pleasure of discovering extreme states of a series of transformations.

D.E. Does modern Japan interest you?

C.L.-S. Of course it does, and besides, it would be impossible to isolate the present from the past. But this interest is only aroused if I can relate the present to the most distant past.

D.E. You don't have the mind of a sociologist?

C.L.-S. More of an anthropologist's, or even an archeologist's. This displeased the students I was with in Korea, who were probably very politicized. I was told that they were saying among themselves, "That Lévi-Strauss, he's only interested in things that no longer exist." And in a sense, it was true.

Also, the natural setting counts for a lot. Japan, a country that we often forget is three-quarters uninhabited, offers spectacles of enormous beauty. Nature in Japan is like nature anywhere else; it presents a series of irregularities to the eye. But in Europe or America, the elements of the composition, I mean the plants and vegetation, are themselves irregular—remember Baudelaire's "the irregular vegetable"? In Japan the diversity of the landscape is the result of the combination of regularly formed plants: cryptomeria, bamboo, tea plantings, rice paddies. The shapes as well as colors provide a denser spectacle, a constant sumptuousness.

In Japan I'm as interested in the trees and the plants as I am in the monuments and the customs. Moreover, isn't that the spirit of the ancient Japanese cults, for which trees and plants, even rocks, are animated beings? One of the reasons Japan fascinates me is the fact that there one feels the presence of a highly developed literary, artistic, and technical culture in direct contact with an archaic past where the anthropologist finds himself on familiar ground.

9

"It Makes the Time Pass"

D.E. From 1964 to 1971, you published the four volumes of the Mythology series.

C.L.-S. It was a time when I got up between five and six every morning, and I didn't know what it was to have a weekend. I really worked.

D.E. The result is vast; several hundred pages a volume, almost two thousand pages in all.

C.L.-S. Mostly I remember the trouble those books gave me. That's even more vast than the result!

D.E. When you finish a book you must feel a certain joy, a real satisfaction.

C.L.-S. Satisfaction that it's over. But I can't say that I write in a happy frame of mind. It is more like anxiety, distaste even. Before beginning, I spend days staring at a blank page before coming up with the opening sentence.

D.E. And when the book is out?

C.L.-S. It's dead, it's over, it has turned into a foreign body. The book passes through me. I'm the place where, for some months or years, things are elaborated or put into place, and then they become separate through some kind of excretion.

D.E. Which of your books do you like best?

C.L.-S. I can't even tell you that. Because if I look at them again, it seems as if someone other than myself has written them. They are not my children.

D.E. Is there a book you would have liked to write or that you regret you didn't write?

C.L.-S. I'm very sorry that I haven't written a literary work.

D.E. A novel or a play?

C.L.-S. I would have liked to be a playwright. No other literary genre seems to me to require as much precision. Each line, each word, must contribute to the action. There must not be any dead wood.

D.E. Have you tried?

C.L.-S. Except for that feeble attempt I mention in *Tristes Tropiques,* no. And that was still a philosophical drama. A well-contrived comedy seems to me to be the pinnacle of the genre!

D.E. On the other hand, you started a novel . . .

C.L.-S. Which I abandoned after thirty pages, it was so bad.

D.E. What was the story?

C.L.-S. It was to be called *Tristes Tropiques.* And it was vaguely Conradian. The plot came from a story I had read in the papers concerning a swindle committed on I don't know what island in the Pacific, in which a phonograph was used to make the natives believe that their gods were coming back to earth. In the book the perpetrators of the fraud would be refugees of various backgrounds, political or otherwise. Different conflicts would arise among them.

D.E. Only the title remains?

C.L.-S. The title and the pages set in italics where I describe a sunset. It was the beginning of the novel.

D.E. Would you have liked to be Joseph Conrad?

C.L.-S. I would have liked to have written his books, at any rate!

*

D.E. In 1983 you published *The View from Afar.* It is a collection of articles compiled in the same fashion as the two volumes of *Structural Anthropology.* Why didn't you call it *Structural Anthropology,* volume 3?

C.L.-S. Because, in the meantime, the word "structuralism" had become so degraded and was the victim of such abuse that no one had any idea what it meant. I continued to know, but I'm not sure that this would have been true of my readers, particularly my French readers. The word lost its content.

D.E. In your preface to the collection, you wrote, "Structuralism was no longer in fashion." Was that nostalgia?

C.L.-S. Of course not. I was making an observation. The educated public in France is bulimic. For a while, it fed on structuralism. People thought it carried a message. That fashion has passed. A fashion

lasts for five to ten years. . . . That's how things go in Paris. I have neither nostalgia nor regret.

D.E. The ebbing of structuralism has been accompanied by a return to more traditional forms of philosophy.

C.L.-S. The two phenomena are interrelated.

D.E. You must deplore this return.

C.L.-S. Why would I do that?

D.E. Because you developed your work against the traditionalist
philosophy.

C.L.-S. That's true, but I don't feel responsible for the salvation of
my contemporaries.

D.E. You're thinking, too bad for them if they're reading that nonsense?

C.L.-S. I wouldn't say "too bad for them," but "good for them if
they're happy reading those books."

D.E. Commentators have marked the end of the structuralist fashion with an exact date, May 1968. You know the phrase, "Structures
don't go out into the streets."

C.L.-S. One thing is certain: May 1968 was the proof that many
developments of the preceding years were founded on misunderstandings. I mean that the interest that educated opinion had in
structuralism was beside the point. Simply because structuralism
was—and continues to be—a type of inquiry far removed from the
major preoccupations of our contemporaries.

D.E. Do you think that the silence of the laboratory is worth more
than the uproar in the newspapers?

C.L.-S. Absolutely.

D.E. Your last book, *The Jealous Potter*—which is a kind of sequel
to the Mythology series—appeared in 1985 and is much more accessible than the others, except for *Tristes Tropiques*, of course. Did you
want to write a more accessible book because you feared that your influence was on the wane?

C.L.-S. First of all, I didn't write the book to be accessible; second,
I don't care much about my influence.

D.E. Still, it is an easier book than the others.

C.L.-S. Yes and no. I begin with no. When the book came out,
many people told me, "Your book is very interesting, but it's terribly

difficult!" I concluded from this that they hadn't opened any of the others. Seeing that this one was smaller and less intimidating, they tried to read it. It discouraged them nonetheless.

D.E. But for someone who has read the others, this one can be approached without any problem.

C.L.-S You're right. Because it is based on older material that I had kept in reserve. I refer to it several times in the Mythology series. I treated it with a certain distance. I was no longer faced with an overpowering mass of data. The books in the Mythology series illustrate the unfolding, almost on a daily basis, of a work of discovery. I labored in a virgin forest that, for me, was an unknown world. I was laboriously clearing a way through barely penetrable thickets and clumps. Writing *The Jealous Potter,* I knew the way out; I could look at things from further away and see them in perspective.

Furthermore, after all the detailed proofs given in the Mythology books, I no longer needed to retrace the various stages of my work. I only had to recall the acquired results, to lay them out on the table, so to speak. I won't hide the fact that, for once, this book was fun to write.

D.E. The book contains some amusing digressions, some little moments of fantasy. . . . I'm thinking of the passage where you compare Labiche and Sophocles.

C.L.-S. I had the idea for a long time. It may even be the distant origin of the book. Moreover, Labiche (whose plays are so badly produced these days) has always delighted me. As a child he was my refuge during our weekly dinners at my paternal grandmother's. I would hide in a corner of her salon with a volume of his complete works and laugh all by myself.

As one moves into old age, bits of the past rise to the surface, or, to put it another way, loops are closed. The Mythology series brought me back to Wagner, whose cult surrounded me when I was a child and who, when I was an adolescent, I thought I had outgrown. *The Jealous Potter* sent me back to the books of my childhood. If the time is given me, I'll undoubtedly once again find *Don Quixote,* which was my passion when I was ten (to amuse our guests, my parents would have one of them open the book at random and start to read; I would go on without any hesitation, for I knew my abridged edition by heart—I can still see the cover, with its slightly glossy pink paper).

Indeed, some people might ask whether I haven't been guided by a
kind of quixotism throughout my career.

D.E. What do you mean by that?

C.L.-S. Not the dictionary definition: a mania for righting wrongs,
becoming the champion of the oppressed, etc. For me quixotism is
essentially an obsessive desire to find the past behind the present. If
perchance someone some day were to care to understand my personality, I offer him that key.

D.E. When *The Jealous Potter* came out, you told me you were
working on another book and it would be the last. Are you still working on it?

C.L.-S. I have the materials before me, but I'm not working on it
much. It would be what they would call in English a "sister book" to
the other. It would be about a problem in mythology parallel to the
one discussed in *The Jealous Potter,* although the myths and the regions of America are different.

D.E. What regions are involved?

C.L.-S. Washington and Oregon. Let's say, the north coast of the
Pacific.

The problem is that I don't know where to begin with all this material, nor above all whether it is truly necessary to add another mythological proof to so many others.

D.E. What will you call the book if you write it?

C.L.-S. One of the things that keeps me from writing it is that I
haven't found a title. It's the title that gives the tone to the work.

D.E. You have written a lot of books, which have been commented
on, discussed, criticized. . . . When you look back, how do they strike
you?

C.L.-S. All that is foreign to me. Someone was talking to me yes-
terday about a problem of mythology, somewhere in South America. I
remember having discussed a similar point. I was asked where; I no
longer knew.

D.E. And your career? You are a doctor *honoris causa* at a great
number of universities throughout the world, you have received the
gold medal from the CNRS, you are a member of the Académie
française. . . . You have received many honors.

C.L.-S. I can't say that I collect them or attach much importance
to them. It happened that I turned down an honorary doctorate. It

was particularly flattering, but I would have had to travel to receive it, and at the time I didn't want to budge.

D.E. So what counts for you are neither the honors nor the fame but the fact of having produced convincing proofs . . .

C.L.-S. I don't delude myself. They are far from convincing to everyone, and they won't remain convincing forever. I'll answer you the way Dumézil was in the habit of doing: In twenty, thirty years, this will seem completely out-of-date.

But you're right. I have the feeling that it will only be possible to treat certain problems better than I have done by referring to what I wrote—even if it is to demolish it; and that my books have signaled a moment in anthropological thought and will be remembered for that.

D.E. Don't you chafe against the thought of being outmoded, even forgotten?

C.L.-S. That would be childish. Centuries of the history of ideas prove that it's everyone's fate.

D.E. But after all that work . . .

C.L.-S. Why did I do it? When I work, I suffer moments of anxiety, but when I don't work I'm bored, and my conscience keeps pricking me. Working doesn't make me any happier, but at least it makes the time pass.

PART 2

THE LAWS OF THE MIND

10

'rs of Marriage

, you were a "structuralist without ~~......., and~~ right away you were able to apply ~~ιιι~~s methods to your work on kinship.

C.L.-S. Things didn't happen that way. I didn't apply his ideas; I became aware that what he was saying about language corresponded to what I was glimpsing in a confused way about kinship systems, marriage rules, and more generally, life in society.

D.E. This was when you began to write *Elementary Structures of Kinship*. In a way it takes up and expands the problems concerning marriage that Marcel Mauss raised in *The Gift* and reinterprets them according to a structuralist method that you found presented in an organized fashion in linguistics.

C.L.-S. If you like. But don't leave out Granet. It was his book, *Catégories matrimoniales et relations de proximité dans la Chine ancienne,* that brought kinship problems to my attention. I read it when I was at the lycée at Montpellier, during the few weeks before my teaching credentials were revoked, and I was spellbound. Granet was dealing with extremely complex systems and attempting to dismantle them, just as one would take apart a piece of machinery, to understand how it was made and how it worked. I discovered an objective way of thinking applied to social facts. And at the same time I was annoyed, because Granet, in his attempt to account for very complex systems, got carried away and imagined solutions that were even more elaborate. In my opinion, simplicity should lie behind complexity. But that is where my whole thinking about kinship systems originates, as well as in some problems I had already encountered in similar material, which I had collected in the field in Brazil.

D.E. *Elementary Structures of Kinship* is an enormous book that opens with several very general chapters, such as the one in which you attack "the archaic illusion" in anthropology.

C.L.-S. You are seeing my thinking in process, and it corresponded to what I was teaching at the Ecole libre des hautes études in New York. I was writing as I went along. I probably needed those preliminaries to formulate my ideas. Today, I'm not so convinced that the overall economy of the book requires them.

D.E. Nevertheless, the first chapter, the one in which you describe the opposition between nature and culture, marked by the incest prohibition, is the basis for everything else in the book.

C.L.-S. It was my starting point. But since then things have evolved.

D.E. Furthermore, in your preface to the second edition, in 1967, you went back to the same point.

C.L.-S. Yes, since the time when I wrote these chapters—around 1943–44—ethology had come into its own and contributed a great deal of new data. Before then we knew of nothing that compared to incest avoidance among animals because, since the time of Aristotle, we had based our reasoning almost exclusively on domestic animals.

Now, observation of animals living in the wild—the great apes, but other species as well—seems to establish that consanguineal unions are rare in these conditions, if not even impossible because of certain regulatory mechanisms. Specialists in this area and ethnologists after them have hastily concluded from this that the incest prohibition has its basis in nature. For some of them, the central thesis of the *Structures* is overthrown; for others, the thesis should be extended beyond human societies to include certain animal societies, such as the vervet monkey, an African species with a long tail, among which the best marriages—I mean the most favorable to the propagation of the species—would be between cousins (the same is true of quail as well), and the members of the species exchange young males with their neighbors. All of this, I admit, leaves me somewhat skeptical. Not concerning the data that have been observed but their interpretation, which too often has an anthropomorphic tinge to it. That there exists a general tendency to expel the young from the group when they reach puberty—sometimes males, sometimes females, depending on the species under consideration—can be explained in various ways, the most likely of which seems to be competition for food. Nothing leads us to think that the dispersion of the young is the result of a so-called incest prohibition in the animal realm. The harmful effects of consanguineal unions—especially when the transfers are made among neighboring groups—would be too weak to explain it.

D.E. So you still maintain the idea stated at the outset of your book, that the incest prohibition shows that the domain of culture is the universe of rules?

C.L.-S. If the incest prohibition were natural in origin, it would be hard to understand why human societies have been obsessed by it and have expended such enormous effort to promulgate it. One could make a compendium of proverbs and sayings among nonliterate peoples revealing the frequency of incestuous desires. And enlarging the problem a bit, have we paid sufficient attention to the endogamous tendencies of traditional European societies? Did you know that in France during the nineteenth century the proportion of marriages contracted within a radius of five kilometers could exceed 80 percent in the countryside? Somewhere Mistral quotes a marvelous Provençal adage that those who support the idea of the natural basis of the incest prohibition would do well to ponder: "Marry within your village; if you can, on your street; if you can, within your house."

As to claims for the lack of sexual desire between individuals who have spent their early childhood under the same roof and the two examples given repeatedly to support them (and that furthermore don't prove a thing)—the kibbutzes of Israel and another case noted in Taiwan—other examples contradict them. Above all, one does not see that this lack of sexual interest within the family circle may be nurtured by the family itself. With your permission, I'll quote Durkheim, who understood this perfectly: "Incestuous relations and family feelings only appear irreducible because we have conceived of the former as irreducibly excluding the latter." Not just us, but the vast majority of societies.

D.E. If you had to rewrite the book today, how would you begin it?

C.L.-S. First of all, I wouldn't write it. As I've gotten older, I have become too prudent to undertake vast synthetic works. I believe all I would need to say is that no matter how great the interest of observations made from animal life and group psychology, the sociological considerations are sufficient to preclude the need for other hypotheses.

D.E. For a first book, it was particularly ambitious.

C.L.-S. You're right. Far too ambitious.

D.E. It was published in 1949 and is still discussed today.

C.L.-S. It was challenged from the first and still is. But the fact that it is an almost obligatory reference in any discussion of the problems is very consoling to me.

D.E. In 1952 Claude Lefort criticized you for presenting the mathematical model as more real than empirical reality.

C.L.-S. I have never claimed that you can reduce the whole of human experience to mathematical models. The idea that structural analysis can account for everything in social life seems outrageous—it has never occurred to me. On the contrary, it seems to me that social life and the empirical reality surrounding it, when seen on a human scale, unfold mostly at random (which is why I defer to history, with its utter unpredictability). I think that in this vast empirical stew, if you'll pardon the expression, where disorder reigns, are scattered small islands of organization. My personal history, the scientific choices I have made, have led to my interest in these aspects rather than in the rest. However, I don't deny the existence of other aspects, and the legitimate interest they may hold. I have chosen for my part to concentrate on areas of inquiry, even though they may be very small, into which it is possible to introduce some rigor, knowing all the while that the cases in question are exceptional. I also know that the type of approach I practice does not exhaust the totality of phenomena—no more, for example, than an elaborate logico-mathematical model of a meteorological conjunction can account for the aesthetic emotion inspired by a sunset. If you want to describe it and analyze it, you have to approach it from a different angle and utilize other modes of understanding.

D.E. Claude Lefort's commentaries in 1952 are rather interesting in that they set off a whole series of criticisms that were to follow you, even hound you, regarding your "formalism," "theoreticism," "abstractionism."

C.L.-S. My answer would be the same.

D.E. Rodney Needham had a different objection. He said that the model reconstructed by analysis or the rule it reveals is not always applied in reality.

C.L.-S. I would go even further: the model is rarely applied as such. Here again it is a matter of knowing what one is choosing to study. It could be the way things happen in the empirical world. Or what goes on in the minds of people who, though failing to observe their own precepts faithfully, state rules for proper conduct. It is this second aspect that I was studying in *Structures*—not what people do, but what they believe or say must be done.

D.E. Pierre Bourdieu, on his part, relies on his anthropological studies of the Kabylie . . .

C.L.-S. Which are quite remarkable . . .

D.E. . . . to challenge your idea of matrimonial "rules" and replace it with the idea of "strategies."

C.L.-S. I'm not surprised at that, because centers of interest shift over time. Sometimes the emphasis is on regulated aspects of social life, at others, on those elements where a certain spontaneity seems to occur. Indeed, there are rules and there are strategies. The strategies can push aside the rules, but it is also unusual, in a given society at a given time, for the strategies used by individuals not to follow certain norms in turn, and so forth. It boils down to knowing what level of observation is the most profitable in the present state of knowledge and in light of a specific inquiry. It will be one or the other, or both at once.

Speaking on a more general level I believe that choices between "this" and "that" prove above all that the so-called social or human sciences are sciences in name only. In true sciences, levels of observation are not mutually exclusive; they complement one another. We have yet to reach that maturity.

D.E. Still, *Structures* visibly made a scientific claim.

C.L.-S. Because it was an effort to clarify a matter in which confusion reigned. For every society, for every custom, there was a bewildering multitude of specific explanations, which I tried to reduce to a few simple principles. It is not science, but at least it is inspired by a scientific outlook.

D.E. While writing the book did you still have the impression you were producing a true scientific demonstration?

C.L.-S. I don't believe that our social and human sciences can ever lay claim to the status of true sciences. At most I tried to take a small step in that direction. For us, the variables are too numerous, the observer inextricably involved with the objects of his observations; finally, since the intellectual means he has at his disposal are of the same level of complexity as the phenomena under study, they can never be transcended.

D.E. In *Structures* you examined a vast number of kinship systems and reduced them to three possible solutions, all founded on two forms of exchange of women. And you added that ideally, according to this plan, it would be possible to construct a chart of a finite number of possible kinship systems. Would you still stand by that analysis?

C.L.-S. Overall, yes, provided we recognize that since that time many systems have appeared in the ethnographic literature that were unknown or lacking sufficient detail when I was writing. They often represent intermediary solutions. This would not lead me to abandon my original system but to make it more complicated and nuanced.

Take for example so-called Arab marriage, that is, marriage that gives preference for a partner to the father's brother's daughter: an endogamous marriage, then, where no exchange takes place between lineages. The exchange, if it does take place, occurs within one lineage, between collaterals. However, for any place for which we have data, this type of marriage represents a minority of cases, and even if we stretch the category a bit (i.e., ignoring the distinction between close and distant female cousins) it never exceeds half of the cases noted, with the others being exogamous. It is as if instead of exchanging their daughters the family exchanges the right to keep some of them, incurring the obligation to give up some of the others. Recently, a number of bright young scholars have shown that things are more subtle still. A tendency for lineages to form constantly higher alliances reestablishes what I once called generalized exchange, in such a way that the kinship relations allowed for marriage purposes, although they remain superficially of the parallel-cousin type are in fact also of the cross-cousin type. It is more complex than the systems I once envisioned, but nevertheless it exhibits the same pattern.

D.E. So kinship systems can be classified on an ideal chart with a finite number of entries?

C.L.-S. For societies with elementary structures, of course. For societies with complex structures, other problems arise. Françoise Héritier-Augé has been able to carry matters further, in a direction I was only able to intimate. In societies where there is no prescribed or preferred marriage pattern, but merely prohibited degrees of consanguinity (as is the case in our own society in simplified form), these prohibitions can be extremely numerous and give rise to genealogical calculations that seem extraordinarily complex. Now, we know, thanks to computers, that these prohibitions operate as if they are the reverse image of what is permitted: the two types of systems, elementary and complex, can each be translated into the language of the other. So they can be unified; their basic structure is the same.

D.E. In your book you speak of women as "signs" that are exchanged, and this has drawn the fire of some feminists.

C.L.-S. They have misunderstood or misread me, for I take pains to state that all human societies look upon their women as values as much as signs. It's a futile argument. One could just as well say that women exchange men; all you have to do is replace the plus sign with the minus sign and vice versa—the structure of the system would not change. If I put it another way, it is only because that is what nearly all human societies think and say.

D.E. Furthermore, it is striking to note that Simone de Beauvoir, in her review of the work in 1949, when she had just published *The Second Sex,* did not contest that point.

C.L.-S. Feminists might take advantage of the way I analyze the myths dealing with the inequality of the sexes, the central theme of *From Honey to Ashes* and *The Origin of Table Manners.* In the first of these books—in the first chapter of the first part, I believe—I form the hypothesis that by mystically subordinating one sex to another, egalitarian societies are already creating blueprints for solutions that will become real but were still impracticable or inconceivable for them at the time, solutions like slavery, that consist in subjecting certain men to the dominion of other men.[1]

---

1. Claude Lévi-Strauss, *Du Miel aux cendres* (Paris: Plon, 1966), p. 244; English edition, *From Honey to Ashes,* trans. John Weightman and Doreen Weightman (New York: Harper and Row, 1973), pp. 285–86.

D.E. In *Elementary Structures* you insisted on the fact that women are not only signs; but nevertheless you refer to matrimonial exchange by comparing it to linguistic or economic exchange.

C.L.-S. Women are not signs, but in the societies in question marriage rules are rules of exchange: the circulation of women establishes communication between biological families.

D.E. At the end of your book, you envisaged developing a generalized theory of exchange and signs.

C.L.-S. A distant prospect, and I was only inviting the reader to think about it.

D.E. Do developments in the biological sciences support this dream?

C.L.-S. To a startling degree. We are learning that everything linguists had taught us about language, everything that seemed its exclusive property exists at the very heart of living matter, that the genetic code and the verbal code exhibit the same characteristics and function in the same way.

D.E. But in a way, these discoveries help eliminate the distinction between nature and culture.

C.L.-S. The distinction still maintains its methodological value. It provides a barrier against those offensives, such as sociobiology, made by simplistic and limited minds, that would have cultural phenomena reduced to models copied from zoology.

If one day the boundary between nature and culture vanishes, it won't be along what we refer to today as the interface between human and animal phenomena, i.e., there where certain human characteristics, such as aggression, seem to resemble what is observed in the behavior of other species. If this change takes place, it will occur elsewhere, involving the most elementary and fundamental mechanisms of life and the most complex human phenomena. If the boundary is to disappear it will be behind the scenes where partisans of culture and nature are presently debating.

D.E. In the last chapter of *Structures*, you mention psychoanalysis and particularly *Totem and Taboo*. You use the term "failure." This is your first debate with psychoanalysis.

C.L.-S. Is it a debate? With *Totem and Taboo* Freud constructed a myth, a very beautiful one at that. But like all myths, it doesn't tell us how things really occurred. It tells us how men need to imagine that things happened in order to attempt to overcome the contradictions they experience in their lives.

D.E. Nearly forty years later, at the end of *The Jealous Potter*, you returned to this debate with psychoanalysis. Your words were as severe as before, though said in a joking manner.

C.L.-S. I don't give the joke any more importance than it deserves. The myths analyzed in *The Jealous Potter*, especially those of the Jivaro, have the peculiar quality that they foreshadow psychoanalytic theories. It was necessary to keep the psychoanalysts from absconding with them and claiming them as a legitimation of their theories. Indeed, it is quite the opposite. Freud's subtitle to *Totem and Taboo* reads, "On some points of agreement between the mental life of savages and that of neurotics." I showed that if the parallels indeed exist, they appear between the mental life of savages, to speak the way Freud did, and that of the psychoanalysts.

D.E. When did you read Freud?

C.L.-S. Very early, for at the lycée I had a friend whose father, a psychiatrist, was one of the first people in France to become interested in Freud. He worked with Marie Bonaparte and urged me to read—I was in the philosophy class—*Introduction to Psychoanalysis*, and the book which at that time, in its first French translation, was called *La Science des rêves*.

D.E. Since then you have often had harsh words to say against psychoanalysis.

C.L.-S. Many of my friends and relatives have tried it. My relationships with them have fed my doubts concerning its therapeutic value. Above all, I wanted to fight the temptation felt by too many anthropologists, sociologists, or historians who, when their interpretations reach an impasse, find it convenient, instead of starting all over, to fill in the gaps with the sort of all-purpose explanations that are especially prevalent in psychoanalysis.

Nevertheless, Freud played a major role in my intellectual development, equal to the role of Marx. He taught me that even phenomena of the most illogical appearance can be subjected to rational analysis. I found Marx's work comparable as it relates to ideologies (which are collective instead of individual phenomena, also essentially irrational): it is possible to reach beyond appearances to find a logically consistent foundation, regardless of the moral judgments one might have with respect to it.

D.E. You remained more faithful to Marx than Freud. At the end of *The Savage Mind*, in 1962, you again proclaim your attachment to Marx.

C.L.-S. Not in a political sense, but from a philosophical standpoint, definitely yes. Marx was the first in the social sciences to use systematically the methodology of models. All of *Capital*, for example, is a model constructed in the laboratory and set in motion by the author so he could view the results in conjunction with observed events. Also, in Marx I found the fundamental idea that one cannot understand what is going on inside people's heads without connecting it to the conditions of their practical existence, something I have tried to do throughout the Mythology books.

D.E. In an article in 1956, Jean Pouillon mentions a book of yours, *Ethnologie et marxisme*. This book never saw the light of day, but can we infer from the title that you were still a Marxist?[2]

C.L.-S. I have often had ideas for books that I did not go on to write. As for my "Marxism," that would be overstating it. Only a few lessons from Marx's teaching have stayed with me—above all, that consciousness lies to itself. And then, as I've already said, it is through Marx that I first glimpsed Hegel, and behind him, Kant. You were asking me about the influences on my work: fundamentally, I'm a common-sense Kantian, and at the same time, perhaps, a born structuralist. My mother told me a story once: when I was still too little to walk and far from knowing how to read, I called out from my stroller one day that the first three letters of the butcher's and baker's signs must mean "bou," as they were the same in the two cases.[3] Even at that age I was looking for invariants!

D.E. What have you retained from Kant?

C.L.-S. That the mind has its constraints, which it imposes on an ever-impenetrable reality, and it reaches this reality only through them.

D.E. That is what you were asserting in a famous passage from *The Savage Mind*, that anthropology is above all a "psychology." This statement might seem paradoxical.

2. Jean Pouillon, "L'oeuvre de Claude Lévi-Strauss," in *Les Temps modernes* 126; reprinted in Lévi-Strauss, *Race et histoire*.
3. *Boucher* and *boulanger.* — TRANS.

C.L.-S. It might seem paradoxical if one reduces anthropology to the collection of objects for museums. But once one sees these objects as thought somehow made concrete, the statement you quote takes on meaning. What we travel thousands of miles to seek, what we look for in our own surroundings, are additional ways of understanding how the human mind works. So we are practicing a type of psychology. And what is true of objects is even more so in the case of beliefs, customs, and institutions.

11

Sensible Qualities

D.E. Perhaps *The Savage Mind* has had its widest influence beyond the circle of anthropological specialists. Your rehabilitation of the primitive mind has been included in every anthology of contemporary thought.

C.L.-S. I wanted to show that there is no gap between the way so-called primitive peoples think and the way we do. When strange customs or beliefs that offended common sense were remarked in our own societies, they would be explained as vestiges or survivals of archaic ways of thinking. On the contrary, it seemed to me that these ways of thinking are always present and alive among us. We often give them free rein. They coexist with forms of thought that take science as their authority, and by that right they are contemporaries.

D.E. For example, your often-quoted comparison between "bricolage" and mythic thinking.

C.L.-S. I gave bricolage as one example of a modality of thinking with its own originality, but to which we pay no attention. Rather, we have no regard for it because it appears futile or secondary; while in reality it reveals essential mental processes and puts us eye to eye with intellectual operations far removed from what we believe to be our modern way of thinking. In the speculative order, mythic thinking operates the way bricolage does on a practical level; it has access to a treasure trove of images accumulated through the observation of nature—animals and plants, with their habitats and distinctive characteristics and their uses in a specific culture. It combines these elements to construct a meaning, just as a bricoleur, faced with a task, uses the materials at hand to give them a different meaning, if I may call it that, than the one for which they were originally intended.

D.E. But this book had a broader epistemological significance.

110

C.L.-S. It was an attempt to go beyond the now classical opposition in Western philosophy between the realm of the sensible and that of the intelligible. Modern science emerged only at the cost of a split between the two, between what in the seventeenth century they called secondary qualities—i.e., the data given by the senses: colors, odors, tastes, sounds, textures—and primary qualities, which could not be attributed to the senses, that form the true reality. Now it seemed to me that the mind of so-called savage peoples is unaware of that distinction and thinks on the level of these sensory qualities; yet on this sole basis it manages to elaborate a vision of the world lacking neither consistency nor logic. And one that is more effective than we believe it to be.

D.E. What you called "the science of the concrete."

C.L.-S. Which seems different from our idea of science, though it is still comparable. This view was strengthened by certain tendencies I noted in contemporary scientific thought. Unfortunately, I have no expertise in scientific subjects. But the traditional natural sciences—zoology, botany, geology—have always fascinated me, like some sort of promised land I will never have the privilege of entering. While I was in the United States I began faithfully reading magazines such as *Scientific American, Science, Nature,* and now *La Recherche.* I have continued the practice. I don't understand it all—far from it. But it gives me food for thought, and I was particularly struck to see that after years of banning secondary qualities and turning its back on sensory qualities, science is now attempting to reintegrate them. Scientists are now asking what is an odor or taste and investigating the shapes of flowers and their evolution, the melodic structure of birdcalls. . . . In this way they often discover the objective basis for popular beliefs and even superstitions.

Unlike Foucault, who makes the point in *Words and Things* that there is a radical rupture between "epistemes," I see contemporary science making an effort to recapture the archaic stages of its development, to integrate very old knowledge into its worldview.

D.E. In order to study this science of the concrete that characterizes the "savage mind," you yourself have acquired an impressive array of concrete knowledge concerning plants, animals, climates . . .

C.L.-S. From the time I began to write *Totemism* and *The Savage Mind* up to the end of the Mythology series, I lived surrounded by books on botany and zoology. Moreover, my curiosity about such matters dates back to my childhood.

D.E. In this case, you have gone beyond the stage of simple curiosity.

C.L.-S. That is true. I had to teach myself in all of these areas. In my office I have as a souvenir an old globe of the heavens. It was a gift from some official organization, I no longer remember which, that I had consulted for information. Astronomers no longer use the instrument, but it has been of great help to me in locating the constellations mentioned in the myths. The scientific knowledge of one or two centuries ago was sufficient for my purposes! I found what I needed in Diderot and d'Alembert's *Encyclopedia,* Brehm's *Zoology,* sometimes even in Pliny . . .

D.E. When you think that some people have criticized you for avoiding the concrete!

C.L.-S. On the contrary, I'm almost obsessive about attending to the minute concrete details.

D.E. Perhaps it's this attention to the concrete that has made you particularly sensitive to the role of the "aesthetic imagination" in the interplay of totemic classifications you describe.

C.L.-S. Yes, because one of the essential differences between the way we think and the way these peoples think is our need to cut things up into pieces. We learned that from Descartes: to divide each difficulty into as many parts as necessary the better to solve it. The way so-called primitive peoples think challenges this division. An explanation is worthwhile only insofar as it is total. When we seek the solution for a particular problem, we look to this or that scientific discipline or else to law, morality, religion, or art. For the peoples studied by anthropologists, all these realms are related. Therefore each expression of collective life forms what Mauss used to call a total social fact. It simultaneously involves all these aspects.

D.E. In *The Savage Mind,* the vocabulary of linguistics is omnipresent. Even more than in *Elementary Structures of Kinship.*

C.L.-S. It provides precious notions, such as that of binary opposition, of marked or unmarked terms. But that is more the vocabulary of relational thought. The nature and importance of my borrowings from linguistics have been misunderstood. Besides being a general inspiration, which, I admit, is enormous, they boil down to the role of unconscious mental activity in the production of logical structures, which was emphasized by Boas, who was an anthropologist as much as a linguist. Second, there is this basic principle that component parts have no intrinsic meaning; it arises from their position. This is true of language, and it is also true for other social facts. I don't believe I have asked anything else from linguistics, and Jakobson, during our conversations, was the first to recognize that I was making an original use of these notions in another area.

D.E. The idea of transformation has a key place in your analyses in *The Savage Mind* as well as in the books in the Mythology series. Where did you find it, in logic?

C.L.-S. Neither in logic nor linguistics. I found it in a work that played a decisive role for me and that I read during the war while I was in the United States: *On Growth and Form,* in two volumes, by D'Arcy Wentworth Thompson, which was first published in 1917. The author, a Scottish naturalist (I inadvertently wrote "English" in *The Naked Man*), interpreted the visible differences between species, or between animal or vegetable organs within the same genera, as transformations. This was an illumination for me, particularly since I was soon to notice that this way of seeing was part of a long tradition: behind Thompson was Goethe's botany, and behind Goethe, Albrecht Dürer and his *Treatise on the Proportions of the Human Body.*

Now, the notion of transformation is inherent in structural analysis. I would even say that all the errors, all the abuses committed through the notion of structure are a result of the fact that their authors have not understood that it is impossible to conceive of structure separate from the notion of transformation. Structure is not reducible to a system: a group composed of elements and the relations that unite them. In order to be able to speak of structure, it is necessary for there to be invariant relationships between elements and relations among several sets, so that one can move from one set to another by means of a transformation.

Another itinerary, better known to historians of ideas, has brought to us the notion of transformation in linguistics; perhaps it also began with Goethe and came down to us by way of Wilhelm von Humboldt and Baudoin de Courtenay. Whatever the area under consideration, the moment one tries to account for diversity by the different ways elements can be combined, the notion of transformation arises.

If I invoke a single principle, the exchange of women between sub-groups of a society, to account for all marriage rules, it is necessary for these rules, which vary according to time and place, to be reducible to stages of the same transformation. The same is true when a linguist draws up the repertoire of phonemes that the vocal apparatus is capable of articulating and discovers the constraints that each language must obey to extract from this common fund the elements of its particular phonological system. The very notion of a phoneme implies that the divergent properties of sounds, as phonetics records them, are optional or contextual transformations of a reality that on a deeper level should be recognized as invariant.

This need, in the fields of linguistics and anthropology, to resort to a notion dating at least from the sixteenth century and derived (with Dürer) from aesthetics and (with Goethe and Thompson) from the natural sciences brought me additional proof that, as I was saying before, scientific thought in its progress does not break with the past but periodically succeeds in reappropriating it.

D.E. Are you still interested today in developments in linguistics?

C.L.-S. Linguistics has become so involved and complicated that I no longer feel capable of following it. The discipline as practiced by Jakobson enthralled me like a detective story. His oratorical talent and sense of the dramatic doubtless had a part in this; but Benveniste had a very different temperament, and reading these two grand masters of structuralism I had—and still do—the feeling of taking part in a great adventure of the mind. In comparison, what is being done today seems arid and tedious.

D.E. Chomsky's generative grammar doesn't interest you?

C.L.-S. I have no doubt of the importance of Chomsky's contribution, which is playing a large role in certain developments of applied linguistics, such as translation machines. However, I confess that this mixture of empirical recipes and scholastic arguments is far from my own way of thinking.

D.E. One could nonetheless say that you have tried to formulate a "generative anthropology," or in any case, in the part of your work dealing with the analysis of myths that you have elaborated a "generative mythology." I believe you even used this expression at one time.

C.L.-S. We both share the idea that the mind generates innumerable combinations with limited means. However, the haste with which philosophers are attempting to draw metaphysical conclusions from Chomskyian linguistics troubles me. Articulated language belongs only to man, agreed. But how does he accomplish this miracle, working by means of a finite number of rules to generate an infinite number of utterances? And can one take it as a reason for the unique place occupied by man in creation?

Formulated by linguists, the first thesis is legitimate even though it remains approximate; the richness of combinations is so great that everything happens in practical terms as if the thesis were true. Nevertheless it is still true that a finite body of rules utilizing a finite vocabulary at a determined moment to generate sentences whose length is not limited but whose probability diminishes to the vanishing point when they become longer and longer can generate only a finite discourse. As in chess, millions of speakers or players will never exhaust the combinations. As for the second thesis, this leap into metaphysics and a certain humanistic mysticism recalls the one made by so many biologists when they give genetic diversity as the proof of the moral duty to respect each human being because of his or her irreplaceable essence. Each human was, is, and will always be unique. So be it. But mankind is not different in this respect from other living beings, even the most humble, which as individuals are also unique; yet man does not believe he has to respect these other beings. Science does not cook up a nice little moral philosophy just to serve us.

12

Philosophers, Science, and the Sioux

D.E. *The Savage Mind* is dedicated to the memory of Maurice Merleau-Ponty . . .

C.L.-S. As a token of my gratitude. I told you about how I entered the Collège de France.

D.E. . . . and the work ends with a chapter of debate with Sartre, about thirty pages that have provoked many reactions since 1962.

C.L.-S. Sartre's *Critique de la raison dialectique* had appeared in 1960, while I was writing *The Savage Mind*. I devoted a year of my seminar at the Ecole des hautes études to a study of Sartre's book. Lucien Sebag assisted me there. He was reading the *Critique* at the same time, and our discussion of it formed a kind of dialogue. Sartre's perspective seemed opposed to that of anthropologists, who view their discipline as one of the ways of understanding the functioning of the human mind; whereas I had the impression that anthropology bothered Sartre, and that he preferred to get rid of it under various pretexts.

D.E. You and Sartre had a lively exchange.

C.L.-S. It wasn't really a debate. To my knowledge, Sartre never responded; except once in an interview, where he confined himself to saying that I hadn't understood anything.

D.E. I believe he responded several times: in the journal *L'Arc*, in 1966, where he declares that you are contributing to the discrediting of history, and in an interview about anthropology, also in 1966, reprinted in *Situations IX*, where he makes a distinction between the anthropology practiced by anthropologists, for whom man is nothing but an object, and the philosophical anthropology that he is trying to elaborate and for which man is "object-subject."

C.L.-S. You know a lot more about it than I do, which shows that I was not taking part in a debate!

D.E. It's true, you didn't return to the question.

C.L.-S. It wasn't important to me. The final chapter of *The Savage Mind* came out of the coincidence of the publication dates of our books.

D.E. Do you think that your book can be read without this chapter?

C.L.-S. Not completely, for I was also laying out my notion of the three types of historical duration, which is very different from Braudel's idea on the subject.

D.E. Your criticism of Sartre was very severe. When you say in *Totemism* that Bergson's philosophy resembles that of the Sioux, people find it amusing, because Bergson no longer seems modern.

C.L.-S. Let's admit that the resemblance is striking. Bergson's text and the words of the Sioux sage that I quote are almost identical.

D.E. Indeed. But it is more difficult to accept the idea that Sartre's philosophy should be considered a contemporary myth and treated as such.

C.L.-S. I'm not putting them in the same category. Bergson ponders metaphysical problems as an Indian might and as in fact the Sioux did. By comparing them I pay homage to Bergson's philosophy, which is rooted beyond time and place in the deepest strata of what is universal in the human mind. For Sartre, it is the opposite. His thought is rooted in an ideology belonging to his own time and intellectual milieu. To situate it in a mythological context, which, in this case, would be that of the French Revolution (for in our society the Revolution of '89 truly has the role of a foundation myth) relativizes Sartre's thought instead of universalizing it.

D.E. One of the problems that Sartre posed was indeed that of the French Revolution and its founding role in our history. You recognize nonetheless that it was an important event.

C.L.-S. That is a weak word. The Revolution put ideas and values into circulation that have fascinated first Europe and then the world and brought France exceptional prestige and influence for more than a century. However, one may wonder if the catastrophes that have struck the West may also find there origin there.

D.E. In what way?

C.L.-S. Because it has given people the idea that society is to be ruled by abstract thought, when instead it is formed of habits and customs; by crushing these in the mortar of reason, one pulverizes ways of life founded on a long tradition, reducing individuals to the state of interchangeable and anonymous atoms. True freedom can be based only on a concrete foundation and is made up of a balance among small adherences, little solidarities. Pitted against these are theoretical ideas proclaimed as rational. When they have achieved their goals, there is nothing left for them but to destroy each other. Today we are observing the result.

D.E. But in what way does wishing to make the Revolution a founding event of the contemporary world seem to you to be a "mythological" attempt?

C.L.-S. In any case, it's an attempt that is still part of this mythology, which was assiduously elaborated throughout the nineteenth century and is being revived on the occasion of the bicentennial.

D.E. And Sartre is heir to it?

C.L.-S. To the extent that he does not offer a concrete image of the events. He builds up an abstract outline of history so that for the humanity of today the French Revolution can play the role of a myth.

D.E. Is Sartre a man of the nineteenth century in your eyes?

C.L.-S. Don't make me attack him. Whatever the charges that can be laid against him, he was a mind of a power that inspires consideration and respect. As for the nineteenth century, it was one of the greatest in scientific, literary, and artistic matters. Who wouldn't want to be a man of the nineteenth century in those areas?

D.E. Your debate with Sartre was emblematic of the polemic between philosophy and the human sciences, which was becoming more heated . . .

C.L.-S. Yes. At least that is how it has been interpreted, even though the last chapter of *The Savage Mind* had a strong philosophical cast.

D.E. In the two replies by Sartre that I mentioned, and in an earlier text by Merleau-Ponty entitled "Philosophy and Sociology," which was reprinted in his book *Signes* in 1960, one truly has the impression that they wished to defend the supremacy of philosophy, which you had just contested.

C.L.-S. Obviously, Merleau-Ponty believed in philosophic thought. He even wished, I told you, to restore the "great philosophy." But there was a difference between him and Sartre: Sartre made philosophy into a closed world. With the exception of the political arena, he was completely uninterested in what was happening outside, especially in scientific matters, to which Merleau-Ponty was on the contrary very attentive. He had a curiosity that Sartre lacked.

D.E. In your opinion does philosophy still have a place in today's world?

C.L.-S. Of course, but on the condition that it bases its reflection on current scientific knowledge and what it has acquired. The "great philosophy," as Merleau-Ponty called it, was the work of men who were the leading scientists of their day. Their philosophical thought was based on their scientific conquests. Today the two functions are separated, but philosophers cannot isolate themselves from a science that not only has immensely enlarged and transformed our vision of life and the world but has overturned the rules of the mind's functioning.

13

The Ragpickers of History

D.E. Your debate with Sartre was not only a confrontation between the human sciences and philosophy. Since you criticized him for overvaluing history, it also raised the problem of the relationship between anthropological thought and history. This is a recurring theme in your work. As early as 1949, you wrote an article called "History and Ethnology," which is reprinted at the beginning of *Structural Anthropology.*

C.L.-S. My criticism of Sartre was not for overvaluing history but for building a philosophy of history that seemed to me, as I was saying a moment ago, to pertain to the order of myth. On my part, nothing interests me more than history—and that has been the case for quite a while!

The article you mentioned was written in 1948. I don't remember if it had been commissioned by the *Revue de Métaphysique et de morale* or if I wrote it on my own. In any event, it was the result of my thoughts upon first reading the works of Lucien Febvre.

D.E. Did you know Febvre?

C.L.-S. Our contacts date from the time I returned to France, in 1948. He had made note of an article I had published in *Renaissance*— the publication of the Ecole libre des hautes études in New York—an article intitled "Split Representation in the Art of Asia and America," which prompted a commentary on his part.[1] As soon as he founded the Sixth Section of the Ecole pratique des hautes études (which later would become the Ecole des hautes études en sciences sociales), he invited me to lecture there.

1. Claude Lévi-Strauss, "Le Dédoublement de la représentation dans les arts de l'Asie et de l'Amérique," in *Renaissance,* vol. 2–3 (New York: 1944–45); reprinted as chap. 13 of *Structural Anthropology,* "Split Representation in the Art of Asia and America." Lucien Febvre, "Emprunts, ou fonds commun d'humanités?" in *Annales* (1951): 380–81.

D.E. In this article, published in 1949, there are some striking remarks: "Everything is history," or again, "Very little history is better
than no history at all. . . ."

C.L.-S. I had been shocked by Malinowski's attitude toward history and what I had observed among some American anthropologists
I knew at the time. Many of them were convinced that it was necessary to go to the field without knowing anything of the population, to
keep one's vision unsullied by any knowledge of its past or information from earlier accounts. That way they believed they were main-
taining the full freshness of direct observation, totally unaware that
all they were doing was impoverishing their experience. All that was
the result of naiveté and sophistry.

D.E. Braudel will make the same comment about you a few years
later. In *Ecrits sur l'histoire* he quotes a sentence from your article "Diogène couché": "an hour spent with a contemporary of Plato's," you
wrote, "would teach us more about the cohesiveness of Greek civilization than all the works of our historians." And Braudel makes the
comment, "Yes, it is true, but only because you would have prepared
for this trip by reading all these works of history."[2]

C.L.-S. It was a jest that Braudel had grounds to criticize. Which
doesn't mean that a five-minute film made in fifth-century Athens
would not completely transform the vision of Greek culture the historians give us. I just said that work in the field must be prepared and
nourished. But there is nothing that can replace it.

D.E. You also state in this article of 1948 that history and anthropology share the same object of inquiry: to understand social life. But
in one case, it is to grasp its conscious expressions, and in the other
to grasp its unconscious expressions. This statement was to receive
ample commentary. . . .

C.L.-S. And be condemned by the historians of the *Annales*
school. They didn't understand that for purposes of my discussion I
was starting off with extreme cases: on the one hand, history as seen
in the most traditional way, with its emphasis on reigns, alliances,
wars, and treaties; and on the other, anthropology as it is practiced
using structural analysis. Now it is true that the first is based entirely
on written testimonies, therefore conscious expressions, and that the

2. Fernand Braudel, *Ecrits sur l'histoire* (Paris: Flammarion, 1969), p. 58.

second seeks to find, behind observed practices, the unconscious mechanisms that govern them.

This opposition disappears in the work of Lucien Febvre and his followers. But this evolution is first of all the result of teachings that Febvre himself extracted from Durkheimian sociology (and from whose somewhat abusive authority he wished to liberate history); and later on it owes a great deal to what anthropology contributed to historians. The "new history," as it is called, has drawn sustenance from anthropology. The whole aim of my article was to show that a destructive and outworn opposition should give way to the work that anthropologists and historians can henceforth carry out side by side in close collaboration.

D.E. And that is what has happened.

C.L.-S. In the last thirty years, a dialogue has grown up between our two disciplines. The historians have understood the importance of the minutiae of daily life that anthropology takes as its substance, details their forerunners tended to ignore. Once while I was in the United States—in 1952, at the anthropological conference organized by the Wenner-Gren Foundation—I said that we were the ragpickers of history sifting through the garbage cans for our wealth. This provoked some stirring in the audience; my colleagues did not appreciate the comparison. At the end of the lecture, Margaret Mead came up to me and said, "There are words that never should be uttered." That day marked the beginning of our friendship, which lasted until her death.

Historians have discovered that this long-neglected refuse lying about in chronicles and memoirs as well as in literature is of the same nature as the observations made in the field by anthropologists, and that they could utilize it.

Around 1950, I was enjoying a series of books by Alfred Franklin, a collection devoted to private life in France from the thirteenth to the eighteenth centuries; from time to time I would find another volume at the bookstalls. There were about twenty in all. Franklin was curator at the Mazarine Library when Proust was employed there for a time; it appears that he never came in. In his own way Proust's boss was also undertaking an admirable remembrance of things past! Even then Franklin's books were an example of what we refer to today as historical anthropology, a speciality popular among historians, as it brings them many readers. For the public—and this is understandable—is more interested in our ancestors' way of life than in that of South American Indians or Melanesians.

D.E. It has sometimes been said that Braudel's article on "the long duration" was written to counter your influence on historians.

C.L.-S. I wouldn't presume to believe it. I imagine he had other and better reasons. However, I admit that at one time that favor anthropology was finding in public opinion might have worried historians. It was a repetition, a few decades later, of the situation of Lucien Febvre with respect to the Durkheim school. In both cases, history was able to preserve its autonomy and be enriched by the contributions of its competitor.

D.E. But on the other hand, historians have contributed a great deal to anthropological research.

C.L.-S. No doubt about it. They have added to the spread of societies in space a temporal dimension, of societies superimposed in time. Consequently, the number of "ready-made" experiences we could base our work on has been substantially multiplied. The result is a strange reversal. In its early days, the *Annales* school had turned away from the old history, that of the chroniclers and memorialists, and became interested in underlying movements of a demographic, economic, or intellectual order, while the anthropologists were taking the reverse route. For it is the history of events, even anecdotal history, that teaches us how matrimonial alliances were concluded, kinship networks formed, inheritances transmitted in noble or royal families as well in traditional peasant milieus. Looking at things from that angle, we were able to uncover points of passage or intersections that enable us to compare far-off and exotic societies with earlier stages of our own. The paths of history and anthropology cross once more, but—it can be hoped—now to follow the same route.

D.E. Still, in this article of 1949 you spoke of the "mind's unconscious activity" that consists of imposing "forms onto a content." And you added that these forms are identical in all societies, whether ancient or modern, primitive or civilized. Such statements have roused historians to criticize you for your ahistorical conception of the functioning of the mind.

C.L.-S. It's a misunderstanding. By restoring the old notion of human nature, I was merely reminding us that the human brain is the same everywhere, and thus identical constraints operate concerning the functioning of the mind. But this mind does not deal with the same problems in all times. Such problems are presented in extraordinarily diverse forms by geographical environment, climate, the state of civilization in which each society is found at a given moment, its ancient and recent historical past; and, for each member of the society, his or her temperament, personal history, position in the group, etc. The machinery is the same everywhere, not the input and output.

D.E. However, there has been talk with regard to you about a "new Eleaticism."

C.L.-S. That's simply absurd, and the historians who have occasionally criticized me for valuing immobility ought to be the first to recognize it. For how could they reconstitute what was going on in the minds of people who lived two, three, or four centuries ago if they did not begin by postulating that there is something in common between us and them and that humans basically think in the same way? If not, the past and the faraway would become equally out of reach. For these historians, this constant is self-evident; they don't see that it poses immense problems that others have the right and duty to consider.

D.E. To avoid the historians' criticisms, you have introduced the distinction between "cold societies," those studied by the anthropologist and lacking a history, and "hot societies," those studied by the historian. But there again, the distinction has raised more problems than it has averted.

C.L.-S. I introduced this idea in *Conversations with Georges Charbonnier*.[3] And I came back to it in my inaugural address at the Collège de France to clear up some misunderstandings. When I speak of "cold" and "hot" societies, I have extreme cases in mind. I have said, written, and repeated a hundred times that no society is absolutely "cold" or "hot." These are theoretical notions that we need in order to frame our hypotheses. Actual societies are distributed along an axis, and none of them occupies either end.

Second, I am not establishing an objective distinction between different types of societies. I am referring to a subjective attitude that human societies adopt vis-à-vis their own history. When we speak of "primitive" society, we put the word in quotes so that people know that the term is

3. Georges Charbonnier, *Entretiens avec Claude Lévi-Strauss* (Paris: Union Générale d'Editions, 1961); reprinted in Collection 10/18 (Paris: Plon-Julliard, 1969); English edition, *Conversations with Claude Lévi-Strauss*, ed. Georges Charbonnier, trans. John Weightman and Doreen Weightman (London: Jonathan Cape, 1969).

improper and has been imposed on us by usage. And yet, in a way, it is suitable; the societies we call "primitive" are not that way at all, but they wish to be. They view themselves as primitive, for their ideal would be to remain in the state in which the gods or the ancestors created them at the origin of time. Of course, this is an illusion, and they no more escape history than other societies. But this history, which they mistrust and dislike, is something they undergo. The hot societies—such as our own—have a radically different attitude toward history. Not only do we recognize the existence of history, we make a cult to it, because—as Sartre's example indicates—we use the knowledge that we desire or believe we have concerning our collective past, or more exactly, the way in which we interpret that past, to legitimate or criticize the evolution of the society in which we live and to direct its future. We internalize our history and make it an element of our moral conscience.

D.E. In a debate with Maurice Godelier and Marc Augé in 1975 published in the journal *L'Homme*,[4] you make a certain number of statements that have been rarely quoted yet give a more precise idea of your conception of history. For example, you say, "It is necessary to bow before the irreducible contingency of history."

C.L.-S. I was repeating the final sentence in *From Honey to Ashes*. When Marxists or neo-Marxists attack me for not knowing history, I answer, You are the ones who don't know it or are turning your backs on it, since in place of history you set up grand developmental laws that exist only in your minds. My respect for history and the taste I have for it originate in the feeling it gives me that no construction of the human mind can replace the unpredictable way in which things really happen. The event in its contingency seems to me an irreducible given. Structural analysis must work with it.

D.E. You reject the idea of "historical laws"?

C.L.-S. There are so many variables, so many parameters, that perhaps only a divine understanding could know or does know what happens and what is going to happen for all eternity. Humans are mistaken at every turn—history proves it. People say, "It's either this or that," and it's always something else.

D.E. Does this absolute contingency leave room for historical analysis?

4. "Anthropologie, histoire, idéologie," in *L'Homme* (July–December 1975): 177–88.

C.L.-S. Of course. Events are unpredictable as long as they have not occurred. But when they take place, one can try to understand and explain them. Events can be connected to one another, and it is possible to grasp the logic of that connection. In the present, there is nothing that makes it possible to predict what, among so many conceivable and inconceivable possibilities, is going to happen.

14

On the Trail of the Bird-Nester

D.E. The Mythology series that you began to publish in 1964 first took form in your courses in the Fifth Section of the Ecole des hautes études.

C.L.-S. Those courses—seminars, really—enabled me to feel my way for several years. I saw how to proceed but was hesitating about getting started. The mythology of the Pueblos first attracted me because of its circumscribed nature and also because of the richness, density, and relative homogeneity of this body of material collected by ethnographers, all American, over a span of a few decades. Lucien Sebag and Jean-Claude Gardin wanted to help me inventory it and put it into shape. At the seminar, we would lay a myth on the table and analyze it together. The results were convincing, but I quickly found the mythology of the Pueblos to be too constricted, too turned in on itself. I needed more room to maneuver so I could test the method. I decided to start over, using the Bororo myth of the bird-nester, which had already attracted my attention in a seminar several years before I began the series.

D.E. In the four volumes of the series you interpret 813 myths plus a thousand variants. And you say that this represents only a small part of the material available. Where do you find these myths?

C.L.-S. Everywhere one can find them. There is hardly a monograph on a people or tribe in which the author, after studying the material culture, family, and social life, hasn't added a few myths. For several populations collections exist devoted entirely to their mythology. I combed through it all for what I needed, for had I begun with a methodical and organized inventory, it would have been ten years before I could have written a word.

D.E. Did you start at random?

C.L.-S. I began with a remark I made a long time ago about the populations I had come to know through my stay in Brazil, that the Bororo and their closest neighbors, members of the Gé linguistic family, have related social organizations whose differences can be interpreted as the stages of a transformation; this hypothesis had been the object of several of my courses and articles. From this a new hypothesis emerged: Could the similarities and differences between the myths of these populations be explained in the same way?

So I began with the mythology of central Brazil, only to realize that, depending on the case, the myths of neighboring peoples coincide, partially overlap, answer, or contradict one another. The analysis of each myth implied that of others, and this semantic contagion, if I may put it that way, spread from neighbor to neighbor in several directions at once. It was as if you arrived at a promontory overlooking a vast territory, which inspired you to reach other spots where your vision extended in new directions.

D.E. This is the method of working outward from the center, which you likened to rose curves rising out of one another?[1]

C.L.-S. The myth taken as the center radiates variants around it, which form the pattern of rose curves that progressively enlarge and become more complicated. And no matter which variant at the edge you choose for a new center, the same thing happens, producing new rose curves that partly overlap with the first and extend beyond them. And so forth, not indefinitely, but until these incurved constructions bring you back to the starting point. The result is that a once indistinct and confused field reveals a network of lines of force and is seen as being powerfully organized.

D.E. This method raises the whole problem of "comparativism." At the end of *The Way of the Masks* you criticize anthropologists who think that one can simply study a single culture, or one culture after another. . . .[2]

C.L.-S. Let's be clear about this. Anthropologists who devote months, years, sometimes decades to the study of a single people deserve all

1. The term refers to a polar curve, $r = a \cos n\,\theta$, listed in H. Martyn Cundy and A. P. Rollett, *Mathematical Models* (Oxford: Clarendon Press, 1952), p. 67. — Trans.

2. Claude Lévi-Strauss, *La Voie des masques* (Paris: Plon, 1979), pp. 145–48; English edition, *The Way of the Masks,* trans. Sylvia Modelski (Seattle: University of Washington Press, 1982).

our gratitude. Without them, we would do and be nothing. The problem arises the moment one wishes to formulate a theory. To do so on the basis of a unique and exclusive experience is fraught with peril, for this experience illustrates only one possible case among hundreds or thousands.

As for the comparative method, it does not, as I have so often said, consist of first making comparisons and then generalizations. Contrary to accepted belief, it is generalization that is the basis for comparison. Faced with a variety of material, one begins by finding a level at which the data that have been observed and described are mutually convertible. And it is only when one has succeeded in formulating these data in a common language, and because of that preliminary sounding, that comparison becomes legitimate.

D.E. To be able to make a comparison, you have to mark off a geographical area where relationships between societies are likely, otherwise . . .

C.L.-S. . . . you fall into the traps that discredited comparativism as it was practiced during the nineteenth century.

D.E. Which implies that you must posit that these peoples whose myths you wish to compare share a common history?

C.L.-S. That is a wise rule, which we owe to Boas. But occasionally, from time to time, we can allow ourselves some wandering. In an article that hasn't appeared at the time we are speaking, as a diversion I compared the way the Bible speaks of circumcision and what the Bororo say about wearing a penis sheath.[3] This risky sort of comparison sometimes leads to ideas that will be better used elsewhere. One can't draw any conclusions, except perhaps that the human mind acts within a limited field of possibilities, so that analogous mental configurations can, without the need for invoking other causes, repeat themselves at different times and in different places. It's a bit like a kaleidoscope, which contains a finite number of translucent fragments; in theory there is nothing to prevent the reappearance of the same pattern after a certain number of turns. It is extremely unlikely, but it is not impossible.

D.E. It is true that the course of your analysis in the Mythology books leads you to find myths that suggest those of ancient Greece.

3. Claude Lévi-Strauss, "Exode sur *Exode*," in *L'Homme* 28 (1988): 106.

C.L.-S. There is a distant resemblance, as there is with some Japanese myths. These likenesses need to be noted in passing, in case possible explanations arise. As a provisional statement, it is enough to admit that the human mind works by using a finite repertoire of formal structures. I leave it to the specialists in these areas of the world to go farther if they can. You undoubtedly know—Dumézil must have spoken to you about it during your interviews with him—that Japanese scholars think they have found the three Indo-European functions in Korea and Japan.[4]

D.E. You are not tempted to think that all these myths are part of a more archaic mythology, common to all, from paleolithic times?

C.L.-S. When you take a general look at universal mythology, here and there you see themes that seem too much alike and too arbitrary to have been independently invented. These similarities could be the result of borrowings that took place relatively recently, relatively a long time ago, or that are extremely archaic. Take a mythological motif such as that of a dwarf-people at war with aquatic birds: we find it in classical antiquity, in the Far East, in America. . . . Was it invented several times? It's highly unlikely. But, then, when and how did it spread? We don't know anything about it. We can imagine anything—that it is a vestigial survival of the mythology of paleolithic times, or that its diffusion is barely a few centuries old and followed routes that some day can be reconstructed. These are special cases, which must be studied individually.

D.E. Your books contain two very different types of comparativism: in *Elementary Structures of Kinship* there is a comparison between continents. While in the Mythology books you assert the need to compare only that which can be brought down to a common history, a shared past . . .

C.L.-S. The goal and the methods of the two inquiries are the same, but the historical situations of each one differ. When I was investigating kinship systems and marriage rules, the literature was full of special explanations. On the contrary, the study of myths remained

4. A tripartite conception of world and society underlying the ideology of most of the Indo-European peoples, which Dumézil termed the three functions: administration of the sacred, physical force, and abundance and fecundity. See, for example, Georges Dumézil, *The Destiny of the Warrior,* trans. Alf Hiltebeitel (Chicago: University of Chicago Press, 1969).—Trans.

the object of a comparativist mania that extended to the whole world and was inspired by superficial resemblances. I had to react in opposite ways.

Also, the two categories of phenomena are on different levels. With kinship and marriage, you are reaching the foundations of social life; it is something like the molecular level, and we know that at that level among living beings things are everywhere the same. Myths offer more complex and diverse aspects, with which one must first come to terms.

D.E. However, your work has sometimes been interpreted as a way to link together all the myths in the world because of your system of "transformations."

C.L.-S. Certainly not. For there is a third difference between the study of kinship and the study of myths. Around 1942–43, when I began to study kinship, I could base my work on a century of systematic studies of kinship systems. I had access to materials that had been described and analyzed in a relatively homogeneous technical language—today we would say, "normalized"—and this made it possible to go on to the next stage, comparison. There was nothing like that for the myths I found in the literature; they were a kind of raw material, barely exploited. So every time I looked at an individual case I had to try to create a language that could possibly be used elsewhere if similar studies concerning other regions of the world confirmed its general validity. Or else they might require other languages analogous to mine, so that the claims to generality would occur at a deeper level. All of this remains to be done; I want to be careful not to prejudice the case.

D.E. Basically, your research method in the Mythology series is rather close to that of Dumézil: to define a geographical area and try to find the same mental structures within it. However, there is a fundamental difference; he had an important historical sequence at his disposal, while you, when you analyze the American myths, cannot find their historical depth.

C.L.-S. I don't need to tell you how much I owe to the work of Dumézil. I learned a great deal and found much encouragement there. But the difference you mentioned is not the only one. Dumézil and I have different goals. He wished to prove that a system of representations, whose presence had been noted in several parts of Asia and Europe, had a common source. For me, on the contrary, the historical and geographical unity was there from the first: America, peopled by successive waves of immigrants who generally all had the same origin and whose entry into the New World took place, according to different authorities, between 70,000 and 15,000 B.P. So I was looking for something else: first of all, to account for the differences between the mythologies whose unity was given by history; and second, starting with an individual case, to understand the mechanisms of mythic thought.

*

D.E. Each volume of the Mythology series is several hundred pages in length. At the end of *The Naked Man,* you consider the work as a homogeneous whole.

C.L.-S. With the reservation that after writing the third volume I told myself that I would never be able to finish because several more were still required. So I decided that I would do only one more, the fourth, and that I would have to put into it, in the form of allusions or invitations to future work, everything else I had to say. Therefore the last volume is thicker than the ones that preceeded it, and of a more complicated construction; it contains the materials for two or three books.

D.E. Did you fear you would fail in your attempt?

C.L.-S. I remembered Saussure and his work on the Nibelungen. He spent part of his life, perhaps most of it, untangling this mixture of myths, legends, and history. All that remains are about a hundred notebooks in manuscript, housed at the library in Geneva, which I obtained on microfilm and studied. Reading this was fascinating, both because of all the ideas I found and because there was a moral there: the inquiry became more and more complicated, new directions kept opening up, and Saussure died before ever publishing anything of his immense labor. I felt exposed to the same danger and resolved to escape it. If not, my own adventure, like his, would never lead to anything.

D.E. When you worked on these myths, your first task was to summarize them. I imagine that they are longer and more diverse than the versions you give.

C.L.-S. I have been wrongly criticized for that. For the details I leave out in the summary I reintegrate into the analysis. It was necessary to allow a reader completely unfamiliar with this mythology, a person for whom America is an unknown world, to begin by acquiring a syncretistic vision of each myth or group of myths. Then I introduce all the details, without omitting a single one, when the analysis makes their role and their necessity plain.

D.E. They are superb stories, true literary works. It must have been an immense pleasure to immerse yourself in this literature.

C.L.-S. They are magnificent stories, often very moving ones. Assuming the informant is also a good storyteller, which isn't always the case. I began to lean toward mythology in 1950 and I completed my Mythology series in 1970. For twenty years, I would get up at dawn, drunk with myths—truly I lived in another world.

The myths filled me up. You have to absorb so much more than you can use. And when you realize that every myth of a given population exists in modified form among a neighboring people, it is necessary to go through the entire ethnographic literature relative to this population to situate any factors that may relate to these modifications in its milieu, its technical knowledge, its history, its social organization. I lived with all these peoples and their myths as if I were in a fairy tale.

D.E. It is also an aesthetic experience.

C.L.-S. And all the more exciting because these myths first seem like puzzles. They tell stories without any rhyme or reason, full of absurd incidents. You have to let the myth incubate for days, weeks, sometimes months, before something suddenly clicks, and in some inexplicable detail of one myth you recognize the transformed detail of another; and by this route they can be brought together. By itself a detail does not have to mean anything, for its intelligibility resides in the differential relationship with other details.

D.E. The titles of your four volumes have become famous. *The Raw and the Cooked, From Honey to Ashes, The Origin of Table Manners* reflect the nature of the whole enterprise, to show the passage from nature to culture. The last one, *The Naked Man* . . .

C.L.-S. . . . goes back to the beginning, for with respect to culture, nakedness is the equivalent of the raw in relation to nature: the first word of the title of the first volume and the last word of the title of the last echo one another, in the same way that a tour beginning in South America and progressively heading northward to the uppermost regions of North America finally returns to its starting point.

D.E. When you called the first volume *The Raw and the Cooked,* did you think of calling the last one *The Naked Man*?

C.L.-S. I wasn't that clear about it. But in general I knew where I was headed. I began with myths that made the invention or discovery of cooking the criterion for the passage from nature to culture. Propelled by the internal logic of the myths and moving from one to the next, I was to end up at myths for which the boundary between culture and nature was no longer between the raw and the cooked but between the acceptance or refusal of economic exchanges, that is, the acceptance or the refusal of a social life extending beyond the boundaries of the group. Fairs or markets, where even enemy peoples periodically gather to exchange food and products of their labor, are the realization of an elaborate form of social life, comparable (and compared by those who are interested) to this initial transformation an isolated culture imposes on nature by cooking its food.

D.E. Along with your "rose curves" your book is organized as a progression from South to North America.

C.L.-S. Indeed, it is in the northwest of North America, from Oregon to British Columbia, that the myths undergo the kinds of transmutations I have just mentioned, due to the exceptional development of commercial exchanges among the tribes. Therefore it was particularly convincing when I found there in scarcely modified form the South American myths I had started out with. There the myths came full circle, joining the two hemispheres as well.

D.E. As you reminded me, your starting point was a Bororo myth about a bird-nester. How do you choose a "key myth" that makes it possible to connect all the others?

C.L.-S. I lived in a Bororo village during my first expedition. My attention was focused above all on social organization; when I was teaching in the Fifth Section and had to concern myself with religious sciences, I also became interested in the mythology that the Salesian missionaries had been gathering for over half a century.

D.E. So you are saying that the choice is completely arbitrary?

C.L.-S. In the beginning, yes. As I was saying about history in general today, in retrospect I can explain and even justify this choice. But when I made it, I did it for accidental reasons.

D.E. In theory, you could have begun with another myth, from another population.

C.L.-S. No doubt, and since the world of mythology is round, another route would have brought me to the same point. However, I understood later on that this myth occupies a strategic position in the totality of Amerindian myths. It joins two systems that concern vertical and horizontal relations respectively: that is, those between high and low, earth and heaven, nature and the supernatural, on the one hand; and on the other, those between near and far, compatriots and foreigners.

D.E. The books on Mythology follow a geographical progression, but the analysis becomes more complex as well.

C.L.-S. That's right. The four volumes progress along a double axis. On the one hand, geographical extension: in *The Raw and the Cooked* the analysis is limited to South America, particularly central and eastern Brazil. *From Honey to Ashes* enlarges the field of action, to the south as much as to the north, but still remains in South America. With *The Origin of Table Manners,* the analysis begins with a myth that is still South American, but from further north, which deals with the same problem but uses different imagery, a kind better illustrated in the myths of North America. So the passage from one continent to the next became necessary, and this book straddles them both. The final volume, entirely North American, leads the reader further. For, by a curious paradox, which I attempt to solve, the most apparent similarities between myths are found between the regions of the New World that are geographically most distant.

The second shift you mentioned is a matter of logic. The myths, as introduced in succession, treat progressively more complex problems. Those discussed in the first volume exploit oppositions between sensory qualities: raw and cooked, fresh and rotten, dry and wet, etc. In the second volume, these oppositions gradually give way to others that no longer appeal to a logic of qualities but to a logic of forms: empty and full, container and contained, inside and outside, etc. The third volume, *The Origin of Table Manners,* makes a crucial step. It deals with myths that, instead of using pairs of opposing terms, set up oppositions between the different ways in which these terms are contrasted: are they conjoined or disjoined? These myths ask how the passage from one stage to the other occurs.

Myths featuring a trip by canoe occupy a strategic position in the book because they provide an admirable illustration of this type of problem. When the voyage begins and as it progresses, what is close becomes far away and the faraway draws near. When one arrives at one's destination, the initial values of the two terms are inverted. But the voyage has taken time. So time is introduced into mythic thought as a necessary way to reveal relationships among relationships previously given in space. This means that a novelistic dimension gradually penetrates the mythic dimension, with all the consequences this implies for the evolution of the two genres. And it also shows that with its increasingly subtle combination of terms that initiated as concrete images taken from lived experience, mythic thought is capable of abstraction, albeit implicitly.

D.E. You show this logical thought, which you described in *The Savage Mind,* in action. In a little digression in *From Honey to Ashes* you ask why peoples who possessed such a capacity for logical abstraction did not make the jump to scientific and philosophical reasoning that took place in other civilizations in ancient times.

C.L.-S. I have no idea. Perhaps for their thinking to be transformed it was necessary for these cultures to change to a different type.

D.E. Concerning Greece, in fact, Jean-Pierre Vernant situates the passage to rational thought in the political organization of the city-state.

C.L.-S. Yes, and others have seen a preliminary condition of scientific thought in the requirements for precision and rigor inherent in juridical thought. These different interpretations are fairly close, it seems.

D.E. Your tour of mythology ends in *The Naked Man* in a chapter intitled, "The Only Myth." You meant that all the myths analyzed throughout the four volumes were in fact only a variation of the same myth?

C.L.-S. Variations on a great theme, at least: the passage from nature to culture, which must be payed for with the definitive breakdown of communication between the heavenly and earthly realms. And the result for humanity is the problems treated by this mythology.

*

D.E. Do you view *The Jealous Potter* as part of the Mythology series? You are dealing with quite a different issue.

C.L.-S. The overall problem is the same. Only the empirical content differs—or aesthetic content, in the Kantian sense of the term. And then, there is a change in tone. The book is shorter and has a faster rhythm. Compared to the Mythology series, *The Jealous Potter* can be seen as having the role of the ballet in the grand operas.

D.E. After having devoted so many years to studying myths, you make this surprising declaration of humility: the science of myths is in its infancy.

C.L.-S. After and even before. In the publicity for *The Raw and the Cooked,* I said that "everything or almost everything remains to be done before we can speak of a true science." And it was over my protests that the publishers of the English translation of the group of four volumes called it "Introduction to a Science of Mythology."

D.E. Still, you have taken a first step.

C.L.-S. I think so, but there are so many more. An upcoming issue of *L'Homme* is supposed to contain an article by my colleague from the Ecole des hautes études en sciences sociales, Jean Petitot, who is a collaborator and disciple of René Thom. [5] There he is translating in terms of catastrophe theory a formula I had presented in 1955 and illustrated with examples in *The Jealous Potter.* I am unable to follow it, but knowing that mathematicians find the formal aspects of my work worthy of consideration and take the analysis of myths seriously gives me great satisfaction.

D.E. Why didn't you try to make the same mathematical formalization in the Mythology books that you undertook in *Elementary Structures of Kinship*?

C.L.-S. From time to time, I have discussed the matter with mathematicians. Some of them have said that it would be possible but too difficult for me, and they had better things to do. The problem raised

5. Jean Petitot, "Approche morphodynamique de la formule canonique de mythe," in *L'Homme* 28 (1988): 106.

in *Elementary Structures of Kinship* was directly related to algebra and the theory of groups of substitutions. The problems raised by mythology seem impossible to dissociate from the aesthetic forms in which they appear. Now these forms are both continuous and discontinuous, an antinomy that catastrophe theory offers a new way to overcome.

One could also think of computers. There have been attempts undertaken abroad to redo *The Raw and the Cooked* by machine, if I may put it that way.

D.E. Do you know what came of it?

C.L.-S. The connections were probably more rigorous, but it took an inordinate amount of time. Doubtless the inventors of these methods also had other things to do; they had managed to generate the first five myths by the time that I, using my old-fashioned methods, had already sketched out a few hundred of them—leaving several of them in a kind of "artistic" blur, obviously.

15

The Workings of the Mind

D.E. I would like to ask a simple question. What is a myth?

C.L.-S. It's the very opposite of a simple question, for it can be answered in several ways. If you were to ask an American Indian, he would most likely tell you that it is a story of the time before men and animals became distinct beings. This definition seems very profound to me. For despite the ink spilled by the Judeo-Christian tradition to conceal it, no situation seems more tragic, more offensive to heart and mind, than that of a humanity coexisting and sharing the joys of a planet with other living species yet being unable to communicate with them. One understands why myths refuse to consider this an original flaw in the creation and see in its appearance the event that inaugurated the human condition and its weakness.

You can also try to define myth in opposition to other forms of oral tradition: legends, tales. . . . But these distinctions are never clear. Perhaps these forms don't play exactly the same role in all cultures, but they are produced by the same sort of mind, and the analyst cannot avoid dealing with them both at once.

What is this mind like? I have already said it. It works by the opposite of the Cartesian method; it refuses to break the difficulty into parts, never accepts a partial answer, and seeks explanations that encompass the totality of phenomena.

When faced with a problem, myth thinks of it as homologous to problems raised in other domains: cosmological, physical, moral, juridical, social, etc. And it aims to account for all of these at once.

D.E. Which explains these sets of Chinese boxes your analysis reveals.

C.L.-S. What a myth says in a language that seems to pertain to one realm spreads to all areas in which a problem of the same formal type may arise.

D.E. That, moreover, is what you note regarding Freud at the end of *The Jealous Potter*. His attention is exclusively fixed on the sexual code.

C.L.-S. We can write infinite epilogues about Freud's ideas. His texts are ambiguous, sometimes contradictory. But it seems beyond a doubt that he gives a key position to the sexual code.

D.E. However, in the myths you analyze, one is struck by the omnipresence of sexuality and the chain of violent acts accompanying it.

C.L.-S. We notice it because this aspect has a large place in our own system of values and social life. Note however that a myth will never deal with a problem pertaining to sexuality in and of itself, isolated from all other issues. It will attempt to show that this problem is formally analogous to other problems that men raise concerning heavenly bodies, the alternation of day and night, the succession of the seasons, social organization, political relations among neighboring groups. . . . When faced with a particular problem, mythic thought sees it as parallel to others. It uses several codes at once.

D.E. It's explanation by means of successive problems.

C.L.-S. Without ever solving any of them. It is the similarity among all these problems that gives the impression that they can be solved, since one becomes aware that the difficulty perceived in one case isn't a difficulty at all in the others or not to the same extent. We reason a bit like that when, asked to give an explanation, we answer with "that's when . . ." or "it's like. . . ." It is laziness on our part, but mythic thought puts this procedure to such a supple and systematic use that it replaces proof.

D.E. Another "simple" question. What is myth for?

C.L.-S. To explain why things, which were different at the beginning, became what they are, and why it could not be otherwise. Because if things changed in one realm, the entire order of the world would be overturned due to the homology among all realms.

D.E. How does myth appear? Some individual must have told it for the first time!

C.L.-S. Of course, but if you take into account the fact that paleontologists are extending the origin of humanity farther and farther into the past, you will agree that the answer to your question is not an easy one. Man's ancestors have probably possessed spoken language for one or two million years, and nothing indicates that they weren't telling each other myths. Over time these myths changed; some disappeared, others were born. Under what conditions? It's a lot like mushrooms—you never see them grow! An individual story does not in itself constitute a myth. For it to become a myth, some kind of secret alchemy must enable the social group to assimilate the story because it answers the group's intellectual and moral needs. Stories issue from the lips of individuals; some succeed, some don't.

The problem of the origin of myths resembles that of the origin of language, which the Linguistics Society of Paris has solemnly forbidden its members to raise because the answers can only be based on conjecture. Perhaps one day neurophysiology will be able to solve the problem. In any case, the answer won't come from either anthropologists or linguists. In the case of mythical representations, it is less interesting to inquire about their origin than people's intellectual attitudes concerning their own myths. There are always different versions of these. Now, people don't choose among these versions, they don't criticize them or decree that one of them is the only true one or truer than the others; they accept them all at the same time, and the differences aren't troublesome. Studies undertaken throughout the world confirm the general nature of this attitude. We should study it up close and compare it with our attitude toward history, in which different and sometimes irreconcilable versions circulate in our societies.

D.E. So, for you a myth is the sum of its variants, its versions. You don't seek to determine the authentic version?

C.L.-S. There isn't a good version, or an authentic or primitive one. All versions must be taken seriously.

D.E. At the end of *The Jealous Potter* you write that myth is a "magnifying mirror" of the way we habitually think. Is that the issue that guided you throughout this long series of books?

C.L.-S. The issue is the same as the one in *Elementary Structures of Kinship,* except that instead of treating sociological facts it deals with religious facts. But the question doesn't change; in the presence of a chaos of social practices or religious representations, will we continue to seek partial explanations, different for each case? Or will we try to discover an underlying order, a deep structure whose effect will permit us to account for this apparent diversity and, in a word, to overcome this incoherence? *Structures* and the Mythology books raise exactly the same problem, and the tactics used are identical.

D.E. But this phrase, "magnifying mirror"?

C.L.-S. In everything I have written on mythology I have wanted to show that one never arrives at a final meaning. Does that ever happen in life? The meaning a myth can offer me, and those who tell it or hear it at such and such a time and under specific circumstances, only exists in relation to other meanings that the myth can offer other narrators or listeners under different circumstances and at a different time.

A myth offers us a grid that is definable only by its rules of construction. This grid makes it possible to decipher a meaning, not of the myth itself but of all the rest—images of the world, of society, of history, that hover on the threshold of consciousness, with the questions men ask about them. The matrix of intelligibility provided by the myth makes it possible to combine them all into a coherent whole. The role I attribute to myth corresponds to the role Baudelaire gave to music. Writing about the prelude to *Lohengrin,* he shows, using examples, that each individual perceives a different content in the work; and nonetheless all these contents can be reduced to a small number of invariant traits.[1]

When we ask in a general way about the meaning of the verb "to mean," we note that it is always a matter of finding a formal equivalent of the meaning we seek in another domain. A dictionary is the illustration of this logical circle. The meaning of a word is given in the form of words whose definition itself relies on other words. And theoretically at least, you come back to where you started, despite the efforts of lexicographers to avoid circular definitions.

We believe we have discovered the meaning of a word or idea when we succeed in finding many equivalents for it from other semantic fields. Meaning is nothing but this use of correspondences. It is true for words and also for concepts. And because myth works by means of images and events, which are manifest to us, it presents this phenomenon in a cruder, more massive way, but one that reflects very general conditions of the workings of the mind.

1. Charles Baudelaire, "Richard Wagner et *Tannhaüser* à Paris," in *Oeuvres complètes* (Paris: Pléiade, 1954), pp. 1211–14.

PART 3

CULTURES AND CULTURE

16

Politics and Race

D.E. In your first course at the Collège de France, you asked questions about the future of anthropology. What would your answers be today?

C.L.-S. I would have to make several alterations, because there has been some evolution during this quarter of a century, and things are not completely the same. Particularly concerning the societies that anthropology studies.

D.E. Because the societies that interest the anthropologist are traditional societies, and they are vanishing one after another . . .

C.L.-S. Did you know that they were saying that back in the eighteenth century? The first scholarly societies founded to study man justified their mission by proclaiming, We must hurry, they won't last much longer. When Frazer, the year I was born, taught his first course at the University of Liverpool, he said the same thing. It is a leitmotiv of anthropological research. I admit that the processes have speeded up and that we can reasonably foresee the end. However, there are still so many things that have been little or poorly studied in the dozens or hundreds of societies that still exist and will continue to exist for a good number of years, that I see a need to intensify our efforts instead of abandoning them. And then, even if we imagine a time when all these cultures have disappeared. . . . Greece and Rome have been gone for a long time, but we continue to study them and offer new views about them.

D.E. But for these cultures we have documents, monuments . . .

C.L.-S. These monuments . . . we are the ones, because of the attention we have paid to them, who have made them so!

D.E. Do you believe it would be as easy to constitute documents or monuments for a small population in Brazil?

C.L.-S. For a population that has been little or poorly studied, or studied over a very short period of time, you are right. The loss will be complete. But—confining myself to America, which I know the best—the collections of the Library of Congress, of the American Philosophical Society, and others abound with manuscripts, many of which have not yet been studied or even catalogued.

D.E. These are forgotten treasures?

C.L.-S. Yes, and they probably represent by their volume as much as Greece and Rome have left us.

D.E. So anthropology is not an endangered science . . .

C.L.-S. It will change its character. If there is no longer an object to fieldwork, we will become philologists, historians of ideas, specialists in civilizations now accessible only through documents gathered by earlier observers. And who knows whether new differences will not appear among a humanity that is in great danger of losing its diversity?

D.E. Do you have the feeling that humanity is heading toward total uniformity?

C.L.-S. Total is too strong a word. But never has it been possible to speak so convincingly of global civilization as it is today.

D.E. Might not anthropology continue to function by taking an interest in contemporary societies closer to us, such as the French countryside?

C.L.-S. Such projects are neither a survival tactic nor a retreat. They have their own intrinsic value. If they are a later development, it is because we had the impression that we knew more about our own societies than we did about exotic cultures; there was a sense of urgency propelling us to study the others. Furthermore, the older stages of our own societies are revealed to us first of all through archives—using the term broadly—that reach back over several centuries. For the societies of central Brazil or Melanesia, 5 to 10 percent of the material we have is historical. The rest of it is the work of ethnographers. In the case of our societies, the proportion is reversed. Here the role of the anthropologist is confined to completing and enriching work that is first of all the task of the historian.

D.E. The future of anthropology is likewise related to institutional matters. Do you think that the situation of the discipline is more satisfactory today than when you first became interested in it?

C.L.-S. When I started out in my career as an anthropologist, there was no such thing as an anthropology chair in any of the French universities. I believe the first person to hold such a position was Marcel Griaule, just before or during the Second World War—I no longer remember. Today anthropology has become a discipline in its own right, taught in the universities. With respect to the urgency of the work remaining to be done, the number of jobs and chairs is still insufficient.

D.E. Like other disciplines, anthropological research must run up against a lack of money—you have to have a budget!

C.L.-S. Except that in the case of physicists or biologists, it is easy to see that they need money to operate their laboratories because that is where they perform their experiments and verify those of their colleagues. It is less readily seen that the laboratories of anthropologists are found thousands of miles away and that they require means to go and live there.

*

D.E. In 1952, with the pamphlet *Race and History,* you departed from a purely anthropological viewpoint to take what could be called a "political" view, a view that dealt with contemporary problems, at any rate.[1]

C.L.-S. I was asked to write it. I don't think I would have written it on my own.

D.E. How did the request come about?

C.L.-S. UNESCO asked several authors to write a series of booklets on the racial question. Leiris was asked, myself. . .

D.E. There you assert the idea of the diversity of cultures, question the idea of progress, and proclaim the need for a "coalition" of cultures.

C.L.-S. Overall, I was looking for a way to reconcile the notion of progress with cultural relativism. The notion of progress implies the idea that certain cultures, in specific times or places, are superior to others because they have produced works that the others have shown themselves incapable of producing. And cultural relativism, one of the foundations of anthropological thought, at least in my generation

1. See chap. 5 n. 1 above.

and the one before it (some are contesting it today), states that there is no criterion that enables one to make an absolute judgment as to how one culture is superior to another. If, at certain times and certain places, some cultures "move" while others "stand still," it is not, I said, because of the superiority of the first, but from the fact that historic or geographical circumstances have brought about a collaboration among cultures, which are not unequal (nothing makes it possible for us to decree them as such), but different. These cultures begin to move as they borrow from others or seek to oppose them. In other periods or in other places, cultures that remain isolated as closed worlds lead a stationary life.

D.E. This has become a classic antiracist document; it is even read in the lycées. Did you write the second article, "Race and Culture," in 1971, as a reaction against this gospel?[2]

C.L.-S. It too was the result of a request from UNESCO, for a conference to open an international year to combat racism.

D.E. Later you said, "This piece caused an uproar, and that was my intent."

C.L.-S. That's perhaps a bit strong. One thing is certain—it did cause an uproar, at least at UNESCO. Twenty years after *Race and History* they asked me to speak again about racism, probably expecting me to repeat what I had already said. I don't like to repeat myself; and above all, much had happened during these twenty years, including my own growing irritation with periodic displays of fine feelings, as if that could suffice. It seemed to me that on the one hand racial conflicts were only getting worse, and on the other there was a confusion about notions such as those of racism and antiracism; because of this carelessness, racism was being fueled instead of weakening.

D.E. This time you spoke of the differences that separate and distinguish cultures from one another. This went against your earlier statements.

C.L.-S. Not at all. When people read the first piece, they read every other line. One critic, I think he was from *L'Humanité,* wanted to prove that I had changed tactics, and quoted a long passage from "Race and Culture" as proof. This passage was in *Race and History.* Since I found it apropos, I had used it again, word for word.

---

2. Claude Lévi-Strauss, "Race et culture"; reprinted as the first chapter of *The View from Afar.*

D.E. Perhaps the most shocking thing about "Race and Culture" was the idea that cultures want to be opposed to one another.

C.L.-S. At the end of *Race and History* I was stressing a paradox. It is differences between cultures that makes their meetings fruitful. Now, this exchange leads to progressive uniformity: the benefits cultures reap from these contacts are largely the result of their qualitative differences, but during these exchanges these differences diminish to the point of disappearing. Isn't that what we are seeing today? Let it be said in passing, this idea that in their evolution cultures move toward a growing entropy that is the result of their mingling—presented in a text which has become, as you were saying a moment ago, a classic document of antiracist thought (I am delighted)—is in direct line with Gobineau, who has been condemned elsewhere as a father of racism. Which goes to show the disorder prevalent in today's thinking.

Moreover, Gobineau's views have a distinctly modern slant, for he recognized that small islands of order may form as the result of what he called—and this is very modern, too—"a correlation of the diverse parts of the structure." He gave examples. Such states of equilibrium achieved among these mixtures, he is aware, buck the tide of a decline he considers to be irreversible.

What can we conclude from all this, except that it is desirable for cultures to retain their diversity or for them to find renewal in diversity? Only—and this is what my second piece was saying—one has to agree to pay the price: to know that cultures, each of which is attached to a life-style and value system of its own, foster their own peculiarities, and that this tendency is healthy and not—as people would like to have us think—pathological. Each culture develops as a result of its exchanges with other cultures. But each must put up some resistance. If not, very shortly there won't be anything unique to exchange. Both an absence and an excess of communication have their dangers.

D.E. How do you explain that your first piece was so successful and the second was not?

C.L.-S. The first was published as a little book. The second was the text of a talk and never appeared on its own. And if in comparison to the second the first has been well received, I can't do anything about it; they form a whole. I will add that the second, in which I attempted to include results of work on population genetics, is more difficult to read. And even with *Race and History,* not a year goes by without lycée students coming to see me or telephoning and saying, We have a report to do and we don't understand a thing!

D.E. What would you do if today UNESCO asked you to give another talk on the same topic?

C.L.-S. There's no chance of that!

D.E. But newspapers and radio stations often ask your opinion on the question of racism, and in general you refuse to answer . . .

C.L.-S. I have no wish to answer because in this area confusion reigns, and, no matter what I say, I know beforehand that it will be misinterpreted. As an anthropologist, I am convinced that racist theories are both monstrous and absurd. But by trivializing the notion of racism, applying it this way and that, we empty it of its meaning and run the risk of producing a result counter to the one we seek. For what is racism? A specific doctrine, which can be summed up in four points. One, there is a correlation between genetic heritage on the one hand and intellectual aptitudes and moral inclinations on the other. Two, this heritage, on which these aptitudes and inclinations depend, is shared by all members of certain human groups. Three, these groups, called "races," can be evaluated as a function of the quality of their genetic heritage. Four, these differences authorize the so-called superior "races" to command and exploit the others, and eventually destroy them. Both the theory and practice are indefensible for a number of reasons that I laid out in "Race and Culture," after or at the same time as other writers did, and with as much vigor as in *Race and History.* The problem of the relationships between cultures is on another level.

D.E. And so, for you, the hostility of one culture toward another is not racism?

C.L.-S. Active hostility, yes. Nothing gives one culture the right to destroy or even oppress another. This negation of the other inevitably takes its support from transcendent reasons: either racism or its equivalent. But that cultures, all the while respecting each other, can feel greater or less affinity with certain others, is a factual situation that has always existed. It is the normal course of human conduct. By condemning it as racist, one runs the risk of playing into the enemy's hand, for many naive people will say, if that's racism, then I'm racist.

You know of my attraction for Japan. When I'm in the metro in Paris and I see a couple that looks Japanese, I look at them with interest and sympathy, ready to give them a hand. Is that racism?

D.E. If you look at them with kindness, no; but if you had said, I look at them with hatred, I would have said yes.

C.L.-S. And nevertheless, I am basing my feelings on physical appearance, behavior, the sounds of the language. In everyday life, everyone does the same in order to "place" a stranger. It would take a lot of hypocrisy to attempt to forbid this type of approximation.

D.E. Are there certain physical appearances that arouse your antipathy?

C.L.-S. Do you mean ethnic types? No, of course not. All of them include subtypes, some of which we find attractive, some not. In some Indian communities in Brazil I felt surrounded by handsome people; I found others presented a sorry sight. Generally the Nambikwara women seemed more attractive than the men; it was the opposite among the Bororo. When we make such judgments we are applying the aesthetic canons of our culture. Under the circumstances the only rules worth paying attention to are those of the parties involved.

Similarly, I belong to a culture that has a distinctive life-style and value system, so cultures that are extremely different don't automatically appeal to me.

D.E. You don't like them?

C.L.-S. That's going too far. If I study them as an anthropologist I work with all the objectivity and even all the empathy I am capable of. That doesn't keep some cultures from fitting in more easily with my own.

D.E. Raymond Aron quotes a letter you wrote to him in 1967 on the subject of Israeli politics: "It is obvious that I can't feel the destruction of the Indians as a fresh wound in my side," you wrote, "and feel the opposite reaction when the Palestinian Arabs are involved, even if (as is the case) the brief contacts I have had with the Arab world have inspired me with a profound distaste. . . ."[3]

C.L.-S. I was exaggerating. I was writing in the heat of the moment, and I didn't want Aron to get the wrong idea about my attitude by attributing pro-Arab sympathies to me. However, it is true that

3. Raymond Aron, *Mémoires*, p. 520.

during a few months I spent in Islamic countries—Pakistan and what today has become Bangladesh—I didn't, as they say, "fit in." I made a confession on the subject in *Tristes Tropiques*.

One day every anthropologist finds himself or herself faced with this sort of situation. Robert Lowie was a great anthropologist who honored me with his friendship. His works on the Crow and the Hopi are authoritative. However, he confided to me that he got along perfectly with the first, while he could hardly stand the second.

D.E. Indeed, when people ask you about racism, it is less about relations among different cultures on different continents than in French society of today and in what is called a "multicultural society." There was even a rumor last year that the government was thinking of asking you to lead a commission entrusted with the task of reforming the laws on nationality, but it abandoned the idea because it might have seemed shocking to ask an anthropologist.

C.L.-S. If what you are saying is true, that's very interesting—the government afraid to shock the immigrants by comparing them to the peoples studied by anthropologists, as if there were an implicit hierarchy among cultures.

D.E. If I am to understand your definition of the term, you judge that in France today there is no racism.

C.L.-S. There are some disquieting phenomena, but except in the case of killing an Arab because he is Arab, an act that should be swiftly and mercilessly punished, they are not a reflection of racism in the true sense of the word. There are and always will be communities inclined to like others whose values and life-styles do not go against their own and who will find others less easy to accept. This does not mean that, even in the second case, relations cannot and should not remain calm. If my work requires silence, and an ethnic community is comfortable with noise or even likes it, I won't blame the community and make accusations about its genetic heritage. Still, I'll prefer not to live too close and will be little appreciative if, on such a spiteful pretext, I am to be found guilty.

D.E. In 1988, can a society be monocultural, given the melting pots of populations, migrations, immigration?

C.L.-S. The term is meaningless, because there never has been such a society. All cultures are the result of a mishmash, borrowings, mixtures that have occurred, though at different rates, ever since the beginning of time. Because of the way it is formed, each society is multicultural and over the centuries has arrived at its own original synthesis. Each will hold more or less rigidly to this mixture that forms its culture at a given moment. Who can deny that, even taking internal differences into account, there is a Japanese culture, an American culture? There is no country more the product of a mixture than the United States, and nonetheless there exists an "American way of life" that all inhabitants of the country are attached to, no matter what their ethnic origin.

Since you are asking me about France, I will answer that in the eighteenth and nineteenth centuries its value system represented something attractive for Europe and beyond. The assimilation of immigrants didn't cause any problems. There would be none today if, from primary school onward, our value system appeared as solid and alive to all as it did in the past.

D.E. All Western societies are clearly encountering this problem of impossible assimilation: England, Germany. . . . The coexistence of cultures in those countries seems as difficult as it is in France.

C.L.-S. If Western societies aren't capable of sustaining or generating intellectual and moral values powerful enough to attract people from outside, people they wish to have adopt these values, then, undoubtedly there is something to be alarmed about.

D.E. Your work, especially the two texts we have just mentioned, has often been seen as parallel to anticolonial movements. What do you think about that?

C.L.-S. I read that from time to time. I even read recently that the success of *Tristes Tropiques* was linked to the rise of the idea of the Third World. That is a misinterpretation. The societies I was defending or for which I was endeavoring to witness are even more threatened by the new setup than they were by colonization. The governments of countries that have won their independence since the Second World War have no sympathy for the "backward" cultures that still exist among them. There is a second reason, which may sound cynical to you: I'm not interested in people as much as beliefs, customs, and institutions. So I defend the small populations who wish to remain faithful to their traditional way of life, away from the conflicts that are dividing the modern world. Those who leave this state and take part in our conflicts cause political and even geopolitical problems; everyone knows that, in this matter, cases of conscience are rarely all on one side.

D.E. Do you distrust the notion of the Third World more than that of decolonization?

C.L.-S. Colonialism was the major sin of the West. However, with respect to the vitality and plurality of cultures, I don't see that we have made a great leap forward since its disappearance.

D.E. Anthropology has been accused of being in collusion with colonialism. Does this view seem well founded to you?

C.L.-S. It is a historical fact that anthropology was born and developed in the shadow of colonialism. However, contrary to the colonial enterprise, anthropologists have sought to protect beliefs and ways of life that cultures were forgetting at an increasing rate.

D.E. Some people have gone so far as to say that anthropology perpetuated colonial domination after the fact. These remarks sometimes come from people who have worked with you, such as Robert Jaulin.

C.L.-S. He was part of the social anthropology laboratory nearly thirty years ago, but we quickly separated because we were incompatible. When native peoples, after undergoing nearly total destruction, wish to reestablish links with their past, it often happens that they rely on books by anthropologists for help. I know quite a few examples of this.

D.E. According to the critics, the Westerner nonetheless maintains his supremacy over the culture he is observing.

C.L.-S. It's not a question of the supremacy of the observer, but of the supremacy of observation. In order to observe, one must be outside. One can—it is an ethical choice—prefer (but is it possible?) to melt into the community whose existence one shares and to identify with it. Knowledge lies on the outside.

D.E. So knowledge only comes from the separation between subject and object?

C.L.-S. It is one aspect. The second time around, one attempts to reconnect them. No knowledge would be possible without a distinction between the two moments; but the originality of ethnographic inquiry consists of this endless switching back and forth.

D.E. In his book on the logic of writing, Jack Goody raises in a fascinating way the problem of relations between the observer and the society under observation; when one studies oral traditions, civilizations that have no writing, the simple fact of transcribing these traditions changes them and imposes the observer's categories of perception and, with them, those of his own culture. Do you have something to say about that?

C.L.-S. The remark seems right, but trivial. This is true of all observation, even in the most advanced sciences. Of course one must remain aware that while transcribing an observation, whatever it is, one is not preserving the facts in their original authenticity; they are being translated into another language, and something is lost in the process. But what can we conclude from it? That one can neither translate nor observe?

*

D.E. A minute ago we spoke of racism. Have you yourself suffered, as a Jew, during your youth or later in your career?

C.L.-S. It would be indecent of me to consider the abominable and overwhelming catastrophe that struck the fraction of humanity of which I'm a part, because I had the luck to escape it. In comparison, the effects I felt were modest: the plundering of my family's possessions, my father's life cut short by the trials of the Occupation . . . however it is clear that it has substantially influenced my fate.

When I was a child, Jewish children were sometimes insulted at the communal school (as it was called then) and at the lycée.

D.E. Have you experienced situations similar to those described by François Jacob in his memoirs? [4]

C.L.-S. Yes, and since I am older than he, I've probably had a few more of them.

D.E. And later on?

C.L.-S. Anti-Semitism may have played a part in one or other career difficulty, but it had a minor role, considering the reservations inspired by my ideas or my person.

D.E. You have always been a partisan of "assimilation" and you have never asserted a Jewish "identity." But you know Métraux's phrase about you, from his journal, "He's the very picture of a Jewish intellectual."

---

4. François Jacob, *Le Statue intérieure* (Paris: Odile Jacob, 1987).

C.L.-S. That doesn't bother me. We're not pure mind, and it seems natural for me, especially as an anthropologist, to size someone up by putting him in his context.

D.E. The phrase doesn't bother you, but what does it mean to you?

C.L.-S. First it would be necessary to know what Métraux meant by it. Our conversations never touched on the subject. I admit that certain mental attitudes are perhaps more common among Jews than elsewhere.

D.E. For example?

C.L.-S. Attitudes that come from the profound feeling of belonging to a national community, all the while knowing that in the midst of this community there are people—fewer and fewer of them, I admit—who reject you. One keeps one's sensitivity attuned, accompanied by the irrational feeling that in all circumstances one has to do a bit more than other people to disarm potential critics. It doesn't upset me if this effort, explicable as it is, gives offense. Gobineau, who wasn't an anti-Semite, described the Jewish mind as that of a seeker by nature, taking pleasure in acquiring "what is science as well as what is gold" from the riches of this world. I imagine Métraux was referring to the first kind of appetite.

D.E. At any rate, you have never asserted or affirmed your Judaism.

C.L.-S. Even for my parents, Judaism was only a memory. I hesitated for a long time before going to Israel, because reestablishing physical contact with one's roots is an awesome experience.

D.E. When did you go?

C.L.-S. In 1984–85. The Israel Musem had invited me to chair an international symposium on art as a means of communication in non-literate societies.

D.E. And what was your reaction?

C.L.-S. I know myself to be Jewish, and the ancientness of the blood, as they used to say, suits me. There more than ever the gap— two thousand years, more or less—between the departure from Palestine and the beginning of the eighteenth century, when I find my ancestors settled in Alsace, frustrated me. What happened in between? The historical sequence, the different stages of this wandering aren't there, and I would need them to be able to perceive the reality of the bond with a far distant past. It is reduced to abstract knowledge. All that is to say that there was no time when I was in Israel that I had the impression of actually touching my roots. Israel has interested me enormously, less because I find it to be a nation of distant cousins (I don't have that kind of family feeling), than as the bridgehead held by the West in the East, the Ninth Crusade, as it were.

D.E. A moment ago I quoted your letter to Raymond Aron in which you compare the situation of the Palestinians to that of the American Indians.

C.L.-S. That is one of those situations—there are others—brought about by history and which have become virtually inextricable, impossible to settle one way or the other in the name of an abstract conception of law or justice.

D.E. In the same letter, you defend General de Gaulle's description of Israel as "sure of itself and dominating," and you condemn the position of the leaders of the French Jewish community, who take advantage, you said, of their privileged positions to circulate propaganda. These are harsh words.

C.L.-S. My letters were written privately, to a friend. When Aron asked me for permission to publish them, I went along with him because I didn't feel I had the right to compromise the balance he wished to give to his work. If I had written for publication, I would have been more careful of how I expressed myself.

Whatever the case, take a look at the text. I was not applying General de Gaulle's phrase to the state of Israel but to the leading Jews of France, who were usurping the right to speak for everyone. All of that is old hat—it has already been twenty years! The massive mobilization of pressure groups had shocked me. Today we have to admit that this mobilization is working in the other direction.

D.E. Your words were harsh, but they were written in private. You haven't made any public statements, and it was necessary to wait until Raymond Aron published an excerpt from your letter to know your position. Don't you like to take a stand in public? As an intellectual you aren't involved in public matters, are you?

C.L.-S. No. I imagine that my intellectual authority, to the degree that I am recognized as having any, rests on the totality of my work, on a scrupulous attention to rigor and precision that, in limited areas, has granted me the right to be heard. If I insist on the right to pronounce on questions I'm unfamiliar with or am ill-informed about, I'm abusing public confidence.

D.E. Do you dislike this figure of the intellectual engaged in public discourse that emerged in France at the time of the Dreyfus affair?

C.L.-S. In the nineteenth century, some intellectuals still lived a tradition that went back to Voltaire. A Victor Hugo could believe himself capable of judging all the problems of his day. I don't think this is possible any more. The world has become too complex, the number of variables that need to be taken into account in each case is immense. Unless one decides to become a specialist in one kind of problem—as with Aron, for example, who has chosen to concentrate on contemporary society. It is a legitimate choice, but it would be impossible to do what he does and what I do at the same time. One has to choose.

D.E. But are you interested in politics? Do you read the papers, watch television?

C.L.-S. Very little television. Otherwise, when would I read? As for the rest, yes, I try to have an educated layman's knowledge of what is going on in politics. I read two dailies, three weeklies.

D.E. An essayist has recently attacked you with some vigor on this very question. He cites your refusal to take a stand on New Caledonia because you have never been there, and he contrasts that with Zola's action in the Dreyfus affair, stating that Zola wasn't competent to make a judgment either, and that didn't keep him from mobilizing for a just cause.[5]

C.L.-S. I'm flabbergasted. Zola not competent about the Dreyfus affair? The moment he found out about it, he was in the forefront! His entire work is devoted to observing, describing, and analyzing contemporary society, to defending the values of truth and justice and making a distinction between honest people and the others. Everything led Zola to respond to the affair with passion; it could have been the subject of one of his novels.

Moreover, what is there in common between the defense of an innocent man and the difficult and painstaking search for an equitable solution of political and economic interests, claims that cannot be repudiated simply with the stroke of a pen? To be informed about such matters one must have a profound knowledge of the people, of the

5. Bernard-Henri Lévy, Le Figaro-Madame, no. 13,300 (June 5, 1987).

setting, of solutions to comparable problems that have arisen in the same part of the world.

Such problems aren't settled by applying a system. An anthropologist has to be particularly careful concerning subjects close to his discipline. I have never been to New Caledonia, nor to the other islands of the South Seas, and I belong to a discipline whose credo is direct observation. If the powers that be had been interested in what I could have to say about New Caledonia, I would have gladly gone there, on the condition of being welcome there. I also would have needed to see what was happening in Samoa, Fiji, and Melanesia.

Shall I make a confession? After *Tristes Tropiques* there were times when I imagined that someone in the press was going to ask me to travel and write. If that had happened, perhaps I would have a clearer notion of contemporary problems.

D.E. It's too bad that no one ever suggested it.

C.L.-S. No, for I wouldn't have written the same books. Whether for better or for worse, I don't know. In any case, it would have been different.

To finish up here, allow me to say that I often intervene in affairs where rightly or wrongly I believe myself to be knowledgeable. But I don't feel I have to broadcast it from the rooftops.

D.E. For example?

C.L.-S. The defense and protection of Amerindian cultures. Last year I went with a delegation to the office of the minister of the Départements d'Outre-Mer to speak about Guiana.

D.E. In the address you made when you entered the Académie française, you quoted a phrase from Montherlant, "What young people need is not an intellectual authority, but someone who can teach them how to act." Don't you like intellectual authorities?

C.L.-S. It is a role that condemns you to misleading your following, unless you're a saint, and then some!

D.E. Sometimes you have been included in the category of intellectual authority.

C.L.-S. Rather, it seems that I heard not long ago that there aren't any more intellectual authorities, which is true.

D.E. You added that Montherlant made a prophetic statement when he said that societies would pay dearly for setting youth apart as a separate entity.

C.L.-S. It's a sign that the present adult generations are no longer sure of their values. I see a kind of abdication on their part.

D.E. Don't you think that an appeal can be made to the young to restore these values?

C.L.-S. Societies maintain themselves because they are able to transmit their principles and values from one generation to the next. The moment they feel unable to hand anything down, or no longer know what to transmit and rely on the following generations, they are sick.

D.E. To end your speech you stated that a radical pessimism like that of Montherlant's is perhaps the only way to give a chance to a moderate optimism. Does this truly reflect your position?

C.L.-S. I've said it often. If we wish to give a kind of moderate humanism a chance, humanity will have to temper its excessive pride and convince itself that its time on earth, which will come to an end in any case, does not give it all rights.

D.E. "And [man's works] were as nothing," are the last words of *The Naked Man* and in a way represent the last word of the Mythology series. They have prompted a great deal of comment about your "pessimism."

C.L.-S. People failed to note, above all, that these last pages were inspired by the conclusion of Gobineau's *Essai sur l'inégalité des races humaines.* I have the book here, let me look. . . . Here it is: "Pausing, even at the times that must shortly precede the last breath of our species, turning our heads away from these ages invaded by death, where the globe, now silent, will continue, but without us, to circle in space in its impassive orbit . . . " and so on. Doesn't that say anything to you? I even wanted to work the word "impassive" into my last sentence, as a kind of "signature" (in the sense of the old alchemists) for Gobineau. There are other disguised quotations in my books.

D.E. Perhaps no one noticed it because this reference might seem paradoxical. Gobineau doesn't have such a positive image, particularly concerning the racial problem. Is he one of your favorite authors?

C.L.-S. As a man, Gobineau was probably steeped in racial prejudices. Many people were at the time. And he didn't make any more of a distinction between race and culture than did others of his day. Let's overlook for a moment those passages where his prejudice overcomes his reason (in others it is the opposite; Gobineau's racism was intermittent, appearing in fits and starts) and agree to read "culture" for "race," and we will see in him, in addition to the very fine writer who was the author of the *Pléiades,* the *Souvenirs de voyage,* the *Nouvelles asiatiques,* and *Trois ans en Asie,* a profound and original thinker. It is he who best understood that readings of history based on different temporal scales don't add up but cancel each other out. I attempted to develop the idea in the final chapter of *The Savage Mind.*

Gobineau's system did not require the first cultures (which, moreover, are theoretical hypotheses) to begin as unequal; it was enough to posit them as different, and that is what he most often did. Only, like all his contemporaries, he was influenced by the West's historical success, and in order to integrate that into his ideas he had to modify his original intuition. If you think about it, it's the same obstacle that even cultural relativism has a hard time overcoming.

D.E. To end a series of books like the Mythology volumes with the disillusioned remark that "nothing" remains of man's enterprises is almost like announcing a philosophical credo. There has been some willingness to see this "nothing" as an expression of your underlying philosophy.

C.L.-S. I didn't say that. I said that man must live, work, think, and keep up his courage all the while knowing that he will not always be here on earth, that one day this earth will cease to exist, and at that time nothing will remain of the works of men. It's not at all the same thing.

My "underlying philosophy," as you call it, runs up against this contradiction and is shaped by it. On the one hand, I put faith in scientific knowledge. Everything I learn from physics or biology enthralls me; nothing gives me more food for thought. At the same time, it seems that every problem we solve or think we've solved brings forth others, and so on, indefinitely. As a result, every day we are faced more and more with the certainty that our capacity for thinking is and will always remain inadequate to account for reality, that the profound nature of this reality will escape our every effort to convey it. Kant is the first to teach us that. But Kant, who had to adjust to man's irremediable incapacity to know the ultimate reality, owing to the antinomies, hoped to ground moral life as an absolute. I'm a hyper-Kantian, if I may use the term, and include within the problem of pure reason moral life, which also has its antinomies that cannot be overcome. And even more so, for if scientific knowledge opens up vistas both immensely great and immensely small, even more dizzying than those imagined by Pascal, it also shows us our insignificance. Let humanity and the earth disappear, and nothing in the cosmos will have changed. And this leads to the ultimate paradox: we aren't even sure that the knowledge that reveals our insignificance has any validity. We know that we are nothing or not much and, knowing that, we don't even know if this truly is knowledge. To perceive that the universe and thought are incommensurate leads us to question the validity of thought itself. It's never-ending.

So, is this the radical skepticism you seemed to be attributing to me? No. For even if we are destined to move from one appearance to the next, it makes a difference to know that sometimes it is wise to stop, and to know where. Somewhere between surface appearance and the exhausting and futile quest for the meaning behind each meaning, several thousand years' experience seems to indicate that there is a middle ground where men find it in their interest to be because there they find more moral and intellectual comfort and feel better or less bad than they do elsewhere, to mention only hedonistic reasons. This is the level of scientific understanding, intellectual activity, and artistic creation. Well, let's hold onto it, and act "as if" resolutely enough to believe in it for all practical purposes, not without occasionally acknowledging, so as to keep our good sense, the memento mori that encompasses both our universe and ourselves.

D.E. Do you see how you have sometimes been accused of "antihumanism"?

C.L.-S. I'll answer that a well-ordered humanism does not begin with itself. By setting mankind apart from the rest of creation, Western humanism has deprived it of a safeguard. The moment man knows no limit to his power, he sets about destroying himself. Look at the death camps and, on another level, with its insidious effects but equally tragic consequences for all of humanity, pollution.

D.E. Some essayists and journalists have recently attempted to link the rejection of a subject-based philosophy with antihumanism and totalitarianism, meaning that only a philosophy of the subject is capable of providing the basis for a politics of the rights of man.

C.L.-S. We have such a mountain of misunderstandings before us that I won't try to clear them up one by one. It would take longer than it is worth. Moreover, I myself devoted some thought to the rights of man in an essay that makes up the final chapter of *The View From Afar*: originally it was a report I made to a parliamentary committee when I was called to testify by the president of the National Assembly.

Without being a philosophy of the subject, or even a philosophy, structuralism can tackle this sort of problem; perhaps it is capable of leaving the beaten path and offering its own answers.

What did I propose? To found the rights of man not, as we have done since the American and French Revolutions, on the unique and privileged character of one living species, but instead to see it as a special case of the rights of all species. By moving in that direction, I said, we would be in a position to obtain a larger consensus than is possible when we confine ourselves solely to the rights of man, since this view has historical links with Stoic philosophy and, at a distance, with the philosophies of the Orient. We would even find ourselves on an equal footing with the practical attitude that "primitive" peoples, the ones studied by anthropologists, have regarding nature. They sometimes lack an explicit theory, but the precepts they observe have the same consequences.

D.E. It is because you reject this endowment of the human species with a privilege over other forms of life, this conversation man has with himself, that you have such harsh words in the "Finale" of *The Naked Man* concerning the philosophy of the subject, consciousness, and so forth.

C.L.-S. Once again, I'm well aware that philosophers may have other interests than my own. Description and analysis can be undertaken on several levels, each of which is legitimate. What I find unbearable in this quarrel about the "subject" is the intolerance of those who remain obedient to a philosophical tradition that goes back to Descartes. Everything begins with the subject, there is nothing but the subject, and so forth. I wanted to see things from another angle, and I don't concede that this right can be disputed.

D.E. At the time, you were challenging traditional philosophy more vigorously.

C.L.-S. Because it claimed it was the only way. One has to fight for one's place in the sun. Let this philosophy agree to being one approach among many, and the conflict evaporates.

17

Literature

D.E. When you express yourself on literature, you often seem to stay away from structuralist literary criticism.

C.L.-S. Criticism that calls itself structuralist. That has used the word "structure" in an arbitrary way and plasters it as a label on any merchandise. I feel like the victim of an intellectual hoax when some critics try, which often happens, to promote the rather poor works they have chosen to study to the rank of masterpieces (because that's where they seek their lessons).

This alleged structuralism is in fact only an excuse for mediocrity. I dwelled on that point in the "Finale" of *The Naked Man*.

D.E. Do you think that works of literature can be ranked according to value?

C.L.-S. If I were to undertake a structural analysis of a literary work, I'd select a poem by Baudelaire, not the lyrics of a popular song.

D.E. That's funny, since a little pamphlet that came out not too long ago has you as one of the instigators of a movement working to eradicate all hierarchies among works of art.[1]

C.L.-S. I haven't read it and know only what the press has said about it.

D.E. But what do you think of the fact that you can be accused of contributing to this eradication because of what you have written on cultural relativism?

C.L.-S. One shouldn't confuse these two meanings of the word "culture." In the generally accepted sense of the word, culture refers to the enlightened enrichment of judgment and taste. In the technical

1. Alain Finkielkraut, *La Défaite de la pensée* (Paris: Gallimard, 1987).

language of the anthropologist, it is something else: according to Tylor's classic definition, which I know by heart because it is so important to us, culture is "knowledge, belief, art, morals, law, custom, and all other capacities and habits acquired by man as a member of society." In this second sense of the term, everything is an object of study: the products that would be considered lower in the first meaning of the word and those that are higher. Cultural relativism confines itself to stating that a culture possesses no absolute criteria authorizing it to apply this distinction to the products of another culture. On the other hand, each culture can and should do that with respect to itself, for its members are both observers and participants.

As a participant in my culture, rock music and comic strips don't attract me at all—to put it mildly! As an observer, I see a sociological phenomenon in the fashion for these two genres that must be studied as such, no matter what judgments one may have concerning their moral and aesthetic value. To idolize the "rock culture" or the "comic strip culture" is to distort one meaning of the word "culture" for the benefit of another, to perpetrate a kind of intellectual swindle. But to take the opposite stand—I mean, to accuse the anthropologist of corrupting the public mind by the mere fact that he has chosen or has been entrusted with this field of study—amounts to the same thing, within reason, of accusing the people who have the highly necessary task of analyzing tissue in biological laboratories of being vampires or coprophiliacs.

D.E. You were speaking of Baudelaire. Were you alluding to the analysis of one of his sonnets that you undertook with Roman Jakobson?[2]

C.L.-S. Yes. One day when he was in Paris, Jakobson told me of his ideas for a structural analysis of poetry. He gave me English, Russian, and German examples, but added that the case of French poetry eluded him. His views so attracted me that I refused to believe that they wouldn't apply to French poetry as well. After he left, Baudelaire's "Les Chats," one of the few poems I know by heart, began running through my head. Little by little there emerged the outlines of

2. "'Les Chats' de Charles Baudelaire," *L'Homme* 2 (1962): 1; Roman Jakobson, *Questions de poétique* (Paris: Seuil, 1973), pp. 401–19; Roman Jakobson, *Selected Writings*, vol. 3 (The Hague: Mouton, 1981): 447–64, 783–85; M. Delacroix and W. Geertz, *'Les Chats' de Baudelaire, Une confrontation de méthodes* (Paris: Presses Universitaires de France, 1980).

an interpretation in the line indicated by Jakobson. I began to work on an analysis that I hardly dare call linguistic, it was so simplistic and clumsy, and I sent Jakobson a letter with the results of my cogitations. He was bursting with enthusiasm, which happened easily with him, and he kept some parts of my analysis, corrected others, and added quite a bit. We exchanged many letters on the subject. When he came back to Paris, we sat down one morning at this desk. I had the pen, and together we edited it all, weighing and discussing every word. It took all day.

D.E. There were no sequels to this episode?

C.L.-S. I'm not a linguist and alone am unable to pursue this sort of experiment. Jakobson went on and published other analyses of poems, all in the same vein.

D.E. Since we're talking about literature, could you tell me who are your favorite writers?

C.L.-S. Conrad, we already spoke of him; Balzac, Chateaubriand . . . Proust, of course. And Rousseau.

D.E. When you mention Chateaubriand, I suppose you have the *Mémoires d'Outre-tombe* (Memoirs from beyond the grave) in mind.

C.L.-S. First of all, yes. But also a book as uneven and often boring as *Génie du christianisme* (Genius of Christianity), where some surprising views are to be found.

D.E. And Balzac? Some chapters of Mythology books are called "Scenes of Private Life" or "Scenes of Provincial Life."

C.L.-S. I must have read him from beginning to end at least ten times, and since my memory is unreliable, each time I reread him, it seems like the first. Not a year goes by without my going back to Balzac.

D.E. Which of his novels is your favorite—*Cousin Pons*?

C.L.-S. There would be dozens of reasons for that choice, but *L'Envers de l'histoire contemporaine* (The Other Side of Contemporary History) captivates me. There Balzac is close to Dickens, whom I also should include among my favorite authors (*Great Expectations* is one of the finest books I know). With Dickens as with Balzac, particularly in *L'Envers,* I hear a tonality I'm particularly sensitive to, the uncanny side of urban life.

D.E. As for Rousseau, should he be included among the writers who have influenced you intellectually?

C.L.-S. I would repeat d'Alembert's remark about Rousseau, "He doesn't convince me, but he stirs me." While I keep aloof from his political thought, the beauty of its construction dazzles me. So I admire Rousseau first of all for aesthetic reasons—what a style! He says in five words what would take me fifteen. And then there are all kinds of considerations that are so complex that I have a hard time sorting them out. Rousseau was one of the first to foresee the future of anthropological research, and he wanted to bring the natural sciences and literature closer together. An uncommon fate made him an observer of acute sensitivity. Throughout his work he seeks the union of the senses with the intellect, which I myself attempt to do by other means and starting from the opposite direction: with the primacy of intellect instead of feeling. But the need for reconciling the two is the same for us both.

During an earlier conversation, I said that Marx was the first to apply the method of using models to the human sciences. Perhaps it would be more fair to give this honor to Rousseau, in the *Discourse on the Origin of Inequality,* even if his models are still too far removed from reality to be connected with it. The *Confessions* make me relive a vanished world, depicted with the same acuity and discreet lyricism of a painting by Chardin or Drolling. Last, *La Nouvelle Héloïse,* which no one reads any more even though it is the first fully modern novel (Mme de Lafayette only created a certain novelistic genre). Remember the story—a girl from a good family has a lover; they marry her to a man older than she is. She tells him everything, and he has nothing more pressing to do than to move the former lover into the family household, thus making everyone unhappy. We'll never know if he acted out of sadism, masochism, in the name of some dubious morality, or simply out of stupidity. The same relationship of the author to his characters, whom he doesn't order about and who, as in life, remain opaque, will appear again, but much later, in Dostoevski and Conrad. And, like the *Reveries,* it is all imbued with an intense feeling for nature. . . . You see, Rousseau stirs me up!

D.E. I was thinking instead about his intellectual influence because the title of one of your lectures, reprinted in volume 2 of *Structural Anthropology,* was "Rousseau, Founder of the Sciences of Man."

C.L.-S. I was stretching it a bit, because of the occasion, a formal ceremony in Geneva for the two hundred and fiftieth anniversary of his birth; but it isn't false.

D.E. There you say that "every ethnologist writes his *Confessions*." Because his work must come out of own ego and depend on it. Yet you have declared you don't have a feeling of personal identity, of ego.

C.L.-S. I don't see any contradiction there. If you don't have this feeling of personal identity, you must work all the harder to regain your self-possession when moving out of exceptional circumstances. Ethnographic experience is an experimental form of research on something which escapes you. If I had a strong idea of who I was, perhaps I wouldn't have needed to go looking for myself in these exotic adventures.

D.E. You don't know?

C.L.-S. Hardly at all.

D.E. Do you think this trait is peculiar to yourself, or is it a human quality?

C.L.-S. I don't pride myself on my singularity. It seems that it is society that imposes the idea of a personal identity upon us. . . .

D.E. And impels someone to sign his books, "Claude Lévi-Strauss, of the Académie française"?

C.L.-S. Yes, that imposes upon you to be someone, to make this "someone" responsible for what he does and says. Without this social pressure, I'm not sure that this feeling of personal identity would be as strong as most people believe.

D.E. To return to Rousseau: it was said, at one time, that you had planned to write a book about him.

C.L.-S. I've thought of it, but if I've sometimes nurtured the idea, I've quickly abandoned it. For two reasons, the first one being that an enormous body of work on the subject has appeared since my student days. To avoid committing gross errors or reinventing the wheel, I would have to go through scores of books that have appeared in the past fifty years. The prospect terrified me.

Second, my relationship to Rousseau is ambivalent. Marx and Freud make me think. Rousseau sets me aflame. The way I perceive it, I would have a hard time making a distinction between the subjective and the objective. I'll add that my attitude toward him has changed. Or at least, the place his works have in my life has changed:

regarding certain aspects at least, let's say his political thought, I have moved away from him since my time as a militant socialist.

D.E. Why?

C.L.-S. *The Social Contract* is a difficult book, perhaps the most difficult in all of political philosophy. As far as I can understand it, I feel removed from this direct relationship between individual and collectivity that he wishes to establish, along with his rejection of any kind of intermediaries existing between the two; for me, it is these intermediaries that give social life its flesh and blood.

18

Painting

D.E. The volumes of the Mythology series are illustrated throughout with drawings, engravings, sketches . . .

C.L.-S. Of two kinds. The myths introduced all kinds of exotic plants and animals. It was necessary to give the reader some illustrations. Most often, I chose old engravings from the time before there was a full divorce between folklore and zoology and botany. I thought it more poetic and likely to elicit a more vivid response from the reader.

On the other hand, it was impossible for me to get a picture of the highly complex transformations I wished to present without manual as well as intellectual work. I built three-dimensional models out of cardboard, paper, and string, many of which were reproduced two-dimensionally in the book. For months, until it fell apart, one of these models, more than a meter tall, hung from the ceiling of the Social Anthropology Laboratory like a kind of Calder mobile.

D.E. The final volume of the series bears an illustration by Paul Delvaux on the cover.

C.L.-S. I've admired his paintings for a long time and often wondered, while studying a myth, how he would have painted it. When, via a third party, I let him know how much I would like him to illustrate the cover of *The Naked Man,* he had the generosity to accept. Oddly enough, the book inspired him to do a very beautiful but realistic composition. His own personal mythology probably didn't intersect with that of the Amerindians.

D.E. We have already spoken of your relationship to painting, which is a function of your family ties. But I would like to come back to the subject of the debate several years ago that followed the publication of your "Le Métier perdu,"[1] in which you made known your grievances against contemporary painting.[2]

C.L.-S. They aren't grievances! Painting from a certain stage of the development of the art is an intimate part of my background and my life history. It is this sort of painting that brings me aesthetic emotion, that sets me thinking. It appeared around the thirteenth century and lasted to the beginning of the twentieth. What has come afterward belongs to a different phase. I admit it moves me rarely or not at all, and I am trying to understand why.

D.E. Would you make it your own, by quoting it, Baudelaire's comment about Manet, "He was the first in the decrepitude of his art"?

C.L.-S. Manet was a great painter. In each of his works there are always stunning parts. At the same time you can see a kind of uncertainty in his canvases, as if they didn't fully reach their goal. At any rate, Manet marks the end of one era and the beginning of another.

D.E. If one hadn't heard your statements about painting, one would readily imagine that the impressionists delighted you.

C.L.-S. But I like them very much. They gave new life to an art threatened with vapidity. They were still very great painters and knew their craft. Notwithstanding, their intolerance with respect to traditional forms of painting as well as the encouragement they gave to a swarm of imitators who had neither their technique nor their talent had a harmful effect. What we owe them lasted no longer than they did, about thirty years.

D.E. Do you think that the "craft" was lost at that time?

C.L.-S. They themselves said so. Monet said that one must paint as a bird sings. In that way they prompted their followers to forget, ignore, and despise craft.

D.E. A moment ago you mentioned your personal history. You once liked modern painting.

C.L.-S. I loved it with a passion. I remember that when we came back to Paris in 1918, after spending the war in Versailles, my father

1. Title given in *Le Débat* 10 (March 1981) to excerpts from a text that would become chapter 19 of *The View from Afar*, "A Meditative Painter."
2. Published in an English version as "To a Young Painter." — TRANS.

wanted to see the exhibits in the galleries and museums. As he was loyal to the traditions of the eighteenth and nineteenth centuries, these visits were disheartening for him. He described cubist pictures to us, and I, barely ten years old, felt it as a revelation—so it was possible to paint without representing anything! I was enchanted. Working with bits of pastels that were lying around the studio, I began to draw what I imagined were cubist works. They had no connection with the real thing. I can still see my naive compositions—everything was flat, two-dimensional, with no attempt to convey volume. But one thing is sure, they didn't represent anything.

A little later, I in turn frequented the galleries on Rue La Boétie. Throughout my entire adolescence, going to see the latest Picassos on display in the windows was a kind of pilgrimage: I went to make my devotions. At the same time, Louis Vauxcelles, a well-respected critic who was friendly with my father and sometimes came to our house, offered to allow me to make my journalistic debut in a little revue he wished to launch (or perhaps re-launch). For my first article, I proposed the subject of the influence of cubism on daily life, which was hardly to Vauxcelle's taste, as he was a sworn enemy of cubism. But he accepted. I began by going to interview Fernand Léger, whom I admired. He received me with extreme kindness. Was the article ever published? I forget.

Even later, around 1929–30, the review *Documents* published a special issue in honor of Picasso, which contained an article signed Georges Monnet, the socialist deputy for whom I served as secretary; I wrote it. Monnet didn't have the time or the interest to do it, so he left it to me.

D.E. What alienated you from modern art?

C.L.-S. I still bow to Picasso's genius. However, today it seems to me that this genius consisted most of all in giving the illusion that the art of painting is still alive. An image comes to mind—on these desolate shores where the shipwreck of painting has cast us, Picasso picks up pieces of the wreckage and plays with them . . .

D.E. Picasso's canvases no longer move you?

C.L.-S. Picasso's work is vast and uneven. There are some astonishingly successful paintings.

D.E. You don't see any kinship between structuralism and cubism?

C.L.-S. It is true—we've discussed it—that cubism could represent, as it did for Jakobson, a means of approaching structuralism. Not as far as I'm concerned. By putting effects of perspective and differences in lighting, or differences of values between contiguous tones, on the same plane, cubism transformed a traditional mode of representation. But all in all, it only replaced one convention with another.

D.E. You stated in your text that the contents of the painting must be external to the painting itself and you praised the inexhaustible richness of nature. So are you condemning any nonrepresentational painting?

C.L.-S. Perhaps it's because of the surrealist influence. Breton never accepted this sort of painting.

D.E. The painter Pierre Soulages made a rather dry answer to your remarks on the "lost craft." He wanted to read into it a kind of proclamation in favor of representational painting.[3]

C.L.-S. I agree with that.

D.E. He makes the objection that the painter's craft doesn't consist in representing something but in working with color.

C.L.-S. For me, the painter's craft doesn't consist in a reproduction but in a recreation of the real. The precision with which the Dutch painters of still lifes of the sixteenth and seventeenth centuries worked to render the texture of a piece of cheese, the downy skin of a piece of fruit, derives its value from the fact that an equivalence arises between physical effects and the intellectual operations implied in the painter's work. In this fashion the painter offers us an intelligible reflection of the material world. He helps us understand it from inside out.

D.E. Soulages also claimed that your admiration extended only to minor nineteenth-century painters!

C.L.-S. That's inaccurate; in *The Savage Mind* I said that, for me, the painter with a capital P, the one who created it all and is responsible for the capital whose revenues painting has lived off of ever since, is Van der Weyden. As with other painters, I ask him to show me reality more clearly than I can see it myself, to help me understand what

3. P. Soulages, "Le prétendu métier perdu," *Le Débat* 15 (September–October 1981).

moves me in the spectacle offered by the world, and to help my faculties feel and know. Or else to bring to me this surreal order of a world once real that now no longer exists. I also wrote an admiring piece on Max Ernst, which shows that I'm not prejudiced against modern painting.

In my interviews with Georges Charbonnier[4] I took as an example Joseph Vernet's series of paintings of the great ports, now located at the Musée de la Marine. This is certainly not second-rate painting. The technique is admirable, the composition, too. By means peculiar to the art, one is transported into a vanished world. And even more marvelous, perhaps this world never existed, for the painter didn't slavishly reproduce what he saw; he rearranged the elements and combined them in a lyrical synthesis. One of Vernet's great harbors is not that far from the evening at the Opéra which Proust described!

D.E. Even more forcefully, Soulages compares your opinion of modern painting to that of totalitarian regimes, because you accuse modern painting of decadence.

C.L.-S. If the totalitarianism is on any side, it would be that of what is called avant-garde painting, with the colossal commercial and political apparatus that prescribes it.

D.E. Aren't you hurt that people can compare your remarks to those made by fascists?

C.L.-S. In the summer of 1987 I read an article in an evening paper that was part of a series, the argument of which went like this— I'm simplifying: in his time, people criticized Rodin's *Balzac,* therefore Buren's columns are beautiful. I'm not about to submit to this type of intellectual terrorism. In addition to the fact that one could reasonably doubt that Rodin's work was well suited to fulfill the function of a public monument, arguments based on authority don't impress me any more if they are formulated straight or inverted.

The Nazis condemned the avant-garde arts in the name of political ideology, and they favored a style of architecture, sculpture, and painting that disgusts me. On the other hand, must I repudiate Beethoven and Wagner because Hitler liked them?

I moved away from avant-garde painting for different reasons—my attachment to an irreplaceable craft, one of the most prodigious ever

4. Georges Charbonnier, *Entretiens avec Claude Lévi-Strauss.*

created by men throughout the millennia and that relies on a certain conception of man's place in the universe. Like many other problems, those raised by art are not one-dimensional.

D.E. There is something of an echo here of what you were saying about the rights of man. Contemporary painting is the outcome of a current that has locked man into a private encounter with himself.

C.L.-S. Yes, the idea that men can draw out of themselves creations that are as valuable or more so than those of nature. Already one of Gauguin's contemporaries, Sérusier, was writing to Maurice Denis that, in comparison to what he had in his head, nature seemed puny and banal. Now, to my thinking, man must persuade himself that he occupies a minute place in creation, that its riches are overflowing, and that none of his aesthetic inventions will ever compete with those offered by a rock, an insect, or a flower. A bird, a beetle, a butterfly invite the same fervent contemplation that we give to Tintoretto or Rembrandt. But our eye has lost its freshness; we no longer know how to look.

19

Music and Voices

D.E. In the "Overture" to the Mythology series you refer to Wagner and present him as the founding father of the analysis of myths. Did you wish to pay homage to music as an art—the four volumes are dedicated to music—or more particularly to the music of Wagner, thus alluding to a closer relation between him and your work?

C.L.-S. Wagner played a capital role in my intellectual development and in my taste for myths, even if I only became aware of that fact well after my childhood, during which my parents used to take me to the Opéra. Not only did Wagner build his operas on myths, but he proposed a way of analyzing them that can be clearly seen in the use of the leitmotiv. The leitmotiv prefigures the mytheme. Moreover, the counterpoint of leitmotivs and poetry achieves a kind of structural analysis, since it works by shifts or displacements to superimpose moments of the plot that otherwise would follow each other in a linear sequence. Sometimes the leitmotiv, which is musical, coincides with the poem, which is literary; sometimes the leitmotive recalls an episode that has a structural relationship to the one happening at the time, either by analogy or contrast.

I only understood that later on, well after I began my analysis of myths, and at a time when I believed myself completely cut off from the spell of Wagnerism. Let's say that I was brooding on Wagner for several decades.

D.E. A relationship to music runs through your whole series, with the first volume beginning with an "overture" and the last ending in a "finale." The chapters of the first volume are composed in the form of "fugues" or "symphonies."

C.L.-S. There are two levels. The first, as you indicate, is the very organization of the chapters. On a deeper level, the whole work deals with the problem of the relationship between these two great modes of expression, music and mythology.

D.E. Can you take that a little further?

C.L.-S. There is a period in Western civilization when mythical thinking weakens and disappears to the benefit of novelistic expression. This split takes place in the seventeenth century. Now, at that time, we witness a phenomenon I believe to be intimately connected with the first: the birth of what is called the great musical form, which seems to reiterate the structures of mythical thought. Modes of thought fallen into disuse as a means of expressing the real are still present in the unconscious and seek new employment. Now they no longer articulate meaning but sound. And because of their former use, it is possible for the sounds thus articulated to acquire a meaning for us.

D.E. Did you have the sense that the mythology whose system you were reconstituting, in North and South America, was an intensely musical mythology?

C.L.-S. If the shift in our civilization that I just described in historical terms could take place, it is because mythic structures prefigured latent musical forms and that, working backward, one can look at the latter to better understand the former. Before coming to life in music, the "fugue" or "sonata" form already existed in myths.

D.E. So, according to you, the musical organization of these books was a necessity. Nevertheless, it diminishes somewhat in the second volume.

C.L.-S. Not at all.

D.E. At any rate, it no longer appears in the chapter titles.

C.L.-S. I wanted it to be clear. Once I had achieved the effect, it was no longer useful to insist on it. It would have seemed pedantic, even clumsy. But the fact that I recapitulate and develop the problem of music in the "finale" is a good indication that the parallel threads of music and mythology run through all four volumes. And besides, it's the final volume that contains the demonstration of the "fugal" form of a myth.

With some strange results. While writing *The Raw and the Cooked,* I hit a roadblock: one mythical transformation, which seemed indubitable, offered a structure for which I was unable to find any musical equivalent. Yet my initial hypothesis required that there be one. I took my problem to René Leibowitz, who was a close friend of mine. He replied that, to his knowledge, no such structure had ever been used musically, although there was nothing to prevent it. A few weeks later he brought over a piece dedicated to my wife and me, which he had just written along the lines I had laid out.

On the other hand, you know that Berio used *The Raw and the Cooked* in his *Sinfonia*. A part of the text is recited, accompanied by the music. I admit that I did not grasp the reason for his choice. During an interview a musicologist asked me about it, and I answered that the book had just come out and the composer had probably used it because it was at hand. Now, a few months ago Berio, whom I don't know, sent me a very disgruntled letter. He had read the interview, several years after the fact, and assured me that the movement of this symphony offered the musical counterpart of the mythical transformations I was revealing. He included a book by a musicologist who had demonstrated the fact.[1] I apologized for the misunderstanding, which was, I said, the result of my lack of musical training, but I'm still baffled.

D.E. One day you said you would have liked to be a conductor.

C.L.-S. If not a composer! Musical creativity has always fascinated me. That the vast majority of men and women are sensitive to music and moved by it and believe they understand it, and yet only a tiny minority are able to create it, haunts me. (This situation doesn't exist in other arts. As children or teenagers we've all tried our hand at writing poetry, and as for the visual arts, remember the ad, "If you can write, you can draw"?) As a child I dreamed of belonging to this minority. I took violin lessons from a violinist at the Opéra who fancied he could teach and whose wife was a pianist. I composed pieces for our little trio, which they had the kindness to play. I believe, heaven forgive me, that at that time I began composing an opera. I got no further than the prelude.

D.E. That's pure Rousseau!

C.L.-S. Except that Rousseau could do it and I couldn't.

D.E. Has music been very important in your life?

---

1. D. Osmond-Smith, *Playing on Words: A Guide to Luciano Berio's "Sinfonia,"* RMA Monographs 1 (London: Royal Musical Association, 1985).

C.L.-S. Enormously. I listen to it all the time, I work in music. This may arouse the ire of some purists, who will accuse me of making music into background noise. But it's more complicated than that, and I would have a hard time explaining the relationship between my work and music except by way of analogy. Why is the nude so important in painting? One would think it is because of the body's intrinsic beauty. I think there is a different reason. Even the most blasé of painters, who is accustomed to working from live models, cannot fail to respond to a beautiful body with a certain erotic excitement. This mild state of tension stimulates and sharpens the artist's perception; he paints better. Consciously or unconsciously, the artist seeks this state of grace. My relationship to music is on the same order. I think better while listening to it. A countrapuntal relationship is established between the articulation of the musical ideas and my own train of thought. Sometimes they go together, sometimes they diverge and then rejoin one another. How many times have I noted— but afterward—that while listening to a work I have stopped hearing. it while an idea has come to me! After this temporary separation, which gives my thinking a kind of autonomy, my thoughts again attach to the work, as if the mental discourse served as a relay for the musical discourse, while at the same time working with it.

D.E. Do you often go to concerts?

C.L.-S. When I was a teenager, I went to the Colonne and Pasdeloup concerts every week, and to others as well. Not any longer, for I have become claustrophobic, and the thought of being imprisoned in a row of seats frightens me. I listen to the radio.

D.E. Don't you like records?

C.L.-S. They unleash another kind of anxiety, temporal instead of spatial. The idea that they are spinning right next to me, approaching their end, that I'll have to get up to change the records . . .

D.E. But behind you I see a recording of the Ring . . .

C.L.-S. Two of them, even—Böhm and Furtwängler. I rarely listen to them.

D.E. You love opera. Is it the voices that move you?

C.L.-S. The voices, and even more the combining and blending of voices. There are some opera ensembles that overwhelm me with delight: the quartet from the first act of *Fidelio,* the sextet from *Lucia di*

Lammermoor, the quintet from *Die Meistersinger,* the final trio from *Der Rosenkavalier.*

D.E. Do you have some particular favorites among opera singers?

C.L.-S. Of course. I kneel in adoration before Elisabeth Schwarz-kopf.

D.E. And not Callas?

C.L.-S. Callas too. Especially when she did Bellini, Donizetti, and Puccini. While I was growing up, my family scorned Puccini: for his verismo, his turgidity, his vulgarity, etc. I only later came to understand his melodic originality (like Richard Strauss, you hear three bars and you know who it is) and the finesse and subtlety of his orchestration. On the other hand, Verdi bores me. I find him pompous and overly ornamental.

D.E. For you, music ends with Debussy, if I'm correct about when you ceased to follow it.

C.L.-S. You stopped too soon. As a teenager I adored all of Stravinsky. Today, I'm more selective: but *Petrouchka, Les Noces,* the Octet for Woodwinds still seem to be musical masterpieces. Music after Stravinsky may interest me and make me think, and I can even be pleasantly moved by the flavor of the tones. It doesn't speak to me.

Epilogue

D.E. When you gave a collection of your articles the title *The View From Afar,* did you intend to express your distance vis-à-vis the society in which we live?

C.L.-S. The title is taken from the Japanese and came to me when I was reading Zeami, the creator of the Noh theater. He says that in order to be a good actor it is necessary to know how to look at oneself the way the audience does, and he uses the expression "seen from afar." I found that it summed up the anthropologist's attitude looking at his own society, not as a member inside it but as other observers would see it, looking at it from far off in either time or space.

D.E. You often say that you are a man of the nineteenth century. What does that mean?

C.L.-S. It's not only my own idea. A few years ago, a young American colleague wrote a book[1] in which he placed me in the tradition of the symbolists and other writers of the period. I have the feeling that if someone waved a magic wand and I were transported to that time without losing my twentieth-century consciousness, I would not feel too far from home. There I would find the seeds of our great inventions before this progress essentially became devoted to creating the remedy for the discomfort it causes.

Let's not make too much of such fantasies. One can't go back to the past. As Stendhal wrote somewhere, one can ardently long for the resurrection of ancient Greece, but the result would be something like the United States (that is, a modern nation) and not the age of Pericles. What we admire the most from the past—literature, art—is

1. James A. Boon, *From Symbolism to Structuralism: Lévi-Strauss in a Literary Tradition* (Oxford: Basil Blackwell, 1972).

181

not what made men happy. The moment they are aware of something else, they hurry to change—take a look at the developing nations.

On the other hand, the idea that the craftsmen of the age of Louis XV, to whom we owe the most exquisite creations of the French genius in the realm of decorative arts, could have been the people who went to view Damiens' execution through hideous tortures for amusement profoundly disturbs me.[2] I think it is a good example because it is close to us, but it is far from being the only one in which there is no incompatibility between artistic refinement and extremely cruel manners. You will have to admit that this raises many questions about man's nature. That's the role of anthropology, you might say. Alas—or perhaps, fortunately—it doesn't have the answers to everything.

2. A man of unsound mind who in 1757 slightly wounded the king with a pocket-knife.—Trans.

Index of Names